CONTENTS

CHAPTER I   Getting Started   1

CHAPTER 2   The Political System of the United Kingdom   7

CHAPTER 3   The Electoral Process for General Elections   15

CHAPTER 4   Political Parties   19

SIX STEPS TOWARDS BECOMING A POLITICIAN

CHAPTER 5   ONE: Education and Training   29

CHAPTER 6   TWO: Building a CV   37

CHAPTER 7   THREE: Work Prior to Entering Politics   49

CHAPTER 8   FOUR: Joining a Political Party   55

CHAPTER 9   FIVE: Gaining Preselection   63

CHAPTER IO   SIX: Standing for Selection   71

CHAPTER II   Managing your image   87

CHAPTER I2   Different paths   91

APPENDIX I   Prime Minister Biographies   92

APPENDIX II   Glossary of terms   95

APPENDIX III   Contacting Your Electoral Commission Office   105

CHAPTER I
GETTING STARTED

INTRODUCTION

Politicians occupy a very special place in our society. As voters, we choose them to make the rules that we all have to live by, and as taxpayers, we trust them to take some of our money and spend it in a way that benefits us all. It's perhaps unsurprising then, that being a politician is not like any other job.

If you're reading this it's because you want to become a politician. Great! But unfortunately, you don't *choose* to be a politician. Instead, you are *chosen* to be a politician. At the end of the day, you have to win an election to become a politician, and that's not something you can totally control. However, you can certainly increase your chances hugely by reading and following the contents of this book.

WHAT IS A POLITICIAN?

Good question! We all know a politician when we see one, but what's the formal definition?

 how2become

The word 'politician' comes from the Greek *polis*, which refers to both a city-state and to a body of citizens. Other English words including policy, polity, police and politics all come from the Greek root *poli* as well.

These days, a politician is someone who is either:

1) *A member of the legislative branch of government.* The legislative branch of government is the assembly (or assemblies) of people who have the power to pass, amend, and repeal laws. That assembly (or those assemblies) are collectively known as the legislature. In the United Kingdom, the legislature is all the members in both Houses of Parliament.

2) *A member of the executive branch of government.* The executive branch is the people who have the authority and the responsibility for the daily administration of the state. When we talk about 'the government' in the United Kingdom as opposed to 'the opposition,' we're talking about the executive branch.

3) *A member of the office of the head of state.* This part of the definition doesn't apply in the United Kingdom, as our head of state (currently Queen Elizabeth) is a nominal head of state who doesn't make decisions. In the United States, for example, the President has an unelected Cabinet of advisors, and they are quite definitely politicians.

NOTE: The political terms and concepts mentioned here will be fully explained during the first chapter, and they also appear in the glossary in the relevant Appendix at the end of this book.

THE PROS AND CONS OF A LIFE IN POLITICS

Every job or profession comes with its own set of pros and

cons. Being a chef is satisfying, but the pay is bad and the hours are terrible. Being a firefighter will make you popular with the ladies, but every time you run into a burning building you risk getting killed. So how does being a politician stack up?

Pros:

1) **Prestige.** Being a politician confers status, attention and prestige. You'll be invited to parties and wined and dined. People will seek you out, court your favour and listen to what you have to say.

2) **The ability to 'make a difference.'** If you have a genuine desire to change society for the better, then entering politics is one (though definitely not the only) way to attempt to do so. Most of us just complain about things we don't like; as a politician you'll have the opportunity to actually take action.

3) **The pay is well above average.** At the time of writing, the annual salary of a Member of Parliament (MP) in the House of Commons was £65,738, and for Cabinet Ministers, £134,565. These amounts are significantly above the national average annual wage for full-time employees of £25,800. In addition, MPs can claim allowances to cover things such as staff costs, travel expenses and the cost of running an office.

Cons:

1) **Your personal life will be affected.** Politicians are public figures, with everything that entails. Your privacy will be affected, people who don't even know you will attack and criticise you, and you'll be held to much higher standards of behaviour, even in your private affairs, than anyone else.

2) ***The hours are long and irregular.*** Standing for election can mean months of 14+ hour days. Once you're elected things aren't quite so bad, but 70 hour weeks won't be uncommon and late nights are normal when bills are being pushed through Parliament. Basically, you'll envy people with 9-to-5 jobs.

3) ***You'll need to spend a significant amount of time away from home.*** It is of course necessary for MPs to attend Parliament in London when the House of Commons sits. Commons typically sits for around 60-70 days in an election year (MPs need time off to campaign in election years), 130-140 days normally, and 200+ days in the year following a general election. If you don't live in London, that's a lot of weeks you'll be travelling back and forth between London and your constituency.

4) ***Job security is nil.*** In politics, your employers (voters) are given the opportunity to get rid of you at regular intervals, and if they choose to do so then your political career might very well be over for good. Politicians in safe seats have much more job security, but safe seats are of course very hard to come by (we'll return to this topic in much more detail later).

5) ***With the same skills and ability you might be able to make more money in private enterprise.*** While MPs get paid well above the national average for full-time work, that's not the whole story. It's entirely possible, indeed likely, that someone who (for example) has a Law degree and the skills to succeed in politics would also be able to do very well financially working as a solicitor or in business. While the national average annual wage is £25,800, the figure for Legal Professionals (for example) is much higher, at £47,411 – and that's just an average.

 how2become

You should take some time to think about these positive and negative aspects of life as a politician and about how they apply specifically to you. We all have different personalities, so for some people the positives will be magnified and the negatives neutralised. For others, the reverse will be the case. Be honest about the sort of person you are, and you'll be able to determine whether a life in politics is the right option for you.

What this book will, and won't, focus on
This book will focus on the question of how to become a Member of the House of Commons of the United Kingdom Parliament. The House of Lords won't be considered, as its membership is not elected.

For reasons of space, this book will not devote any specific attention to the devolved parliaments of Scotland, Wales and Northern Ireland. It also won't devote attention to the European Parliament. Also, and again for reasons of space, this book will not devote attention to running for local government office.

BACKGROUND INFORMATION
You might have decided that you want to become a politician. But do you understand clearly what a politician does? How the political system works? What part the political parties play? All of this is necessary background knowledge for the would-be politician, and so it's presented here.

NOTE: This part contains a lot of political terms, some of which you might not be familiar with. Usually these words will be explained in the text, but if not, you'll be able to find definitions for them in the glossary in the relevant Appendix at the end of this book.

CHAPTER 2
THE POLITICAL SYSTEM OF THE UNITED KINGDOM

INTRODUCTION

If you want to become a politician, you'll need to become a student of the political system in order to give yourself the best possible chance of success. This chapter is intended to give you a good grounding in the United Kingdom's political system, touching on all of the aspects of it that might be relevant to someone who wants to become a politician.

WHY DO WE HAVE GOVERNMENTS?

Let's begin our examination of the political system with something of philosophical question: why do we have governments? After all, governments cost a lot of money to run and sometimes they stop us doing what we want – why don't we just keep the money that we'd otherwise pay in taxes and do things for ourselves?

According to political theory, one reason we pay taxes and submit to the authority of the government and its institutions is that it makes for a fairer society. With no police and no judicial system, only people who are strong, rich and/or powerful would be able to protect themselves from other people who might want to steal from or harm them. Without free healthcare and financial assistance for the poor, life would be miserable for everyone who is unable, for whatever reason, to earn a decent living.

Another reason to have governments is that there are things we all want (roads, hospitals, a military to protect us) but are unable to coordinate and cooperate with each other enough to get. Governments solve this coordination problem: they take some of our money in the form of taxes and spend the money, theoretically at least, on these things that we all want.

While these arguments in favour of having governments are only theoretical (we don't know exactly what would happen if we decided to dispense with our governments), they are strong ones, because we can see that many negative consequences flow from situations in other countries where the government and its institutions are weak or corrupt. Then again, there are some people who argue persuasively that we would be better off with much smaller (and therefore cheaper) governments than we currently have. What do you think? Whatever the arguments for and against, our governments are of course here to stay, but that's no reason not to consider the issue and arrive at your own conclusions.

LEVELS OF GOVERNMENT

In most of the United Kingdom there are only two levels of government: Central Government and the various local governments. In England however, there is an additional

third level of government in between those two: the regional governments.

Let's take a look at these three levels of government and what they do.

Local Governments

Local governments (also known as local authorities) look after local affairs such as roads, transport, education and housing. Their sphere of influence is limited to a certain defined physical area. For example, the London Borough of Enfield is a local government district. It covers an area of 82 km2 and shares borders with the London Boroughs of Barnet, Haringey and Waltham Forest, as well as the Hertfordshire districts of Broxbourne and Welwyn Hatfield, and the Essex district of Epping Forest.

In total there are 433 local authorities in the United Kingdom. Of these, 353 are in England, 26 are in Northern Ireland, 32 are in Scotland and 22 are in Wales.

Local authorities are run by councils. Councils are made up of elected councillors and paid officials. Many councils also have an elected mayor, but decisions are made by the whole council. Councillors are elected every four years and most of them are representatives of a political party.

Local authorities get most of their money from Central Government. The rest is from local taxes such as Council Tax. The money that local authorities spend amounts to about a quarter of total government spending in the United Kingdom. The majority of this goes on education and social services.

The Central Government Department for Communities and Local Government is the main link between Central Government and the local authorities.

Regional Government

Sitting between Central Government and the local authorities in England (but not in Northern Ireland, Scotland or Wales) are nine regional governments. The regions are: East Midlands; East of England; Greater London; North East England; North West England; South East England; South West England; West Midlands, and Yorkshire and the Humber.

Only the Greater London region has a directly elected administration. The other regions have what are called Local Authority Leaders' Boards. They have limited powers and functions delegated to them by Central Government departments, with members appointed by local government bodies.

London has what is called the London Assembly. It's comprised of 25 members who are elected at the same time as the Mayor of London. Its main job is to scrutinise the activities of the Mayor. Of the 25 members, 11 are elected on a London-wide basis and the other 14 are elected as Constituency Assembly members, each representing a separate area of London made up of two or three of the 33 London Boroughs.

Central Government

On to the main game. The Central Government is the United Kingdoms' national government. It looks after national affairs, such as health, defence, foreign policy and the environment, and it has the power to make laws for the whole country.

NOTE: The remainder of this chapter is about Central Government, not local or regional government.

Our System of National Government

Different systems of national government exist. For example, in the United States of America they use a presidential system. This is where the executive (in this case, the President) is separate from the legislature (Congress). The President of the United States is not a member of Congress.

In the United Kingdom we use a parliamentary system of government. This is where the members of the executive – the Prime Minister and Cabinet, also known as 'the government' – are drawn from the legislature. The Prime Minister and the senior ministers who make up the Cabinet are also members of Parliament.

Another feature of the parliamentary system is that the executive is answerable to Parliament. A successful vote of 'no confidence' in Parliament will force the government either to resign or to dissolve Parliament and call a general election. However, due to the existence of political parties (which we'll cover much more in a later chapter), this is a very unlikely scenario.

The United Kingdom Parliament

Parliament, which sits in the Palace of Westminster in London, has three main roles: to debate and pass new laws; to examine and challenge what the government does, and to enable the government to raise taxes.

Laws made by parliament are known collectively as legislation (this distinguishes them from judge-made law). Before a piece of legislation passes into law it's known as a bill.

The United Kingdom Parliament is 'bicameral,' meaning that it consists of two chambers: the House of Commons and the House of Lords.

The House of Commons is a democratically elected body of 650 members, known as 'Members of Parliament' (MPs). MPs are elected through the first-past-the-post system by electoral districts known as constituencies (more on the electoral process in the next chapter). They play a role in Parliament, but they are also supposed to represent the people of the area that elected them, and act in their

interests. MPs hold their seats until Parliament is dissolved, which must happen within a maximum of five years of the preceding election.

Members of the House of Lords are not elected. Instead, its members are made up of two groups: the 'Lords Spiritual' and the 'Lords Temporal.' The Lords Spiritual are the 26 senior bishops of the Church of England. They hold office by virtue of their ecclesiastical role in the church. The Lords Temporal make up the rest of the membership. The majority of the Lords Temporal are life peers, appointed by the Monarch on the advice of the Prime Minister. At the time of writing (2010), the House of Lords had 707 members, 57 more than the House of Commons.

The once-powerful House of Lords has been severely curtailed by statute and by practice, and so today the House of Commons is by far the more powerful chamber.

With the exception of money bills (that is, bills solely concerning taxation or government spending), a bill can be introduced in either House, but it's much more common for bills to be introduced in the House of Commons.

The role of the executive

We've already mentioned that the executive branch of government in the United Kingdom consists of the Prime Minister and the Cabinet. You will have noticed that the executive is also (and in fact more commonly) called 'the government.' Because this is confusing, we'll stick with calling them the executive as much as possible in this book for reasons of clarity.

While the members of the executive are Members of Parliament, the Parliament and the executive are separate institutions. Unlike Parliament, the executive actually runs the

country. It has responsibility for developing and implementing policy and for drafting bills, which then go to the Parliament for debate and eventually a vote on whether or not they will pass into law.

CHAPTER 3
THE ELECTORAL PROCESS
FOR GENERAL ELECTIONS

INTRODUCTION

In the United Kingdom, the elections for the MPs who will form the House of Commons are known as general elections. If you hope to become an MP, a close study of the working of the electoral process for general elections is (for obvious reasons) a very good idea!

FREQUENCY OF ELECTIONS

General elections in the United Kingdom are held about every four years (the average length of Parliament since 1945 has been three years and seven months.). The reason that the interval between elections is not exact is that the Parliament Act 1911 says only that parliamentary sessions last a maximum of five years. Therefore elections are not fixed, and the exact date of each election is chosen by the sitting government to maximise political advantage.

CONSTITUENCIES

General elections are actually made up of 650 individual elections that take place on a single day, all across England, Wales, Scotland and Northern Ireland. Why are there 650 individual elections? It's because for the purposes of the political system, the United Kingdom is divided into (currently 650) geographic areas of broadly equal population. These areas are called 'constituencies.'

CANDIDATES

The elections that are held in each constituency are to elect an MP to the House of Commons, one per constituency. As there are currently 650 constituencies there are 650 currently sitting MPs.

The people standing for election are called candidates. In order to get people to vote for them, they campaign in their constituency. They announce a set of ideas they say will guide them when making decisions if they are elected, and they may even announce specific things that they will try to do to improve life in the constituency if elected.

On polling day every eligible resident can vote for one of the candidates standing for election in their constituency. The candidate with the most votes in each area wins a place, or 'seat,' in the House of Commons, and thereby becomes an MP.

ELECTORAL SYSTEMS

As we mentioned earlier, the electoral system used for general elections in the United Kingdom is first-past-the-post. This is a very simple system: each voter votes once, for one candidate, the votes are counted and the candidate with

the most votes wins. This kind of electoral system is the one that's most commonly used in everyday life – for example, to elect the president of a club or sporting association – so most of us are familiar with it. It's very intuitive and if someone asked you how an election works, the first-past-the-post system is probably what you'd describe.

That being said, it's possible to conduct an election in a myriad of different ways, and first-past-the-post is just one of them. This is worth mentioning, because while the first-past-the-post system is intuitive and sounds fair, it attracts significant criticism. The main criticism of the first-past-the-post system is that it can ignore the fact that most of the voters preferred a candidate other than the winner.

Let's look at this in more detail. Say for example there are three candidates in an election: Candidate A; Candidate B, and Candidate C. Now let's say that on polling day, the votes fall as follows:

Candidate A – 45%

Candidate B – 38%

Candidate C – 17%

Under the first-past-the-post system, Candidate A would win the election. However, note that a majority of the voters (38% for Candidate B + 17% for Candidate C = 55%, which is more than half) actually preferred someone else. Is fair or correct then that Candidate A should win?

Now suppose that the second preference of the 17% who voted for Candidate C would have been Candidate B. That is, if they could not have Candidate C, they would have preferred Candidate B to Candidate A. If you eliminated Candidate C on the basis of the first poll and then everyone

voted again, Candidate B would get a winning majority of 55%. This scenario makes the election of Candidate A under the first-past-the-post system seem even less fair and correct.

We'll see in the next section that the idiosyncrasies of the first-past-the-post system are particularly important when the existence of political parties is considered, and consequently, highly relevant to your goal of becoming a politician.

There is currently a campaign in the United Kingdom for 'electoral reform,' meaning a consideration of other electoral systems possibly leading to a switch. If you want to become a politician, you'd be wise to follow this debate closely and consider the ramifications should there be a switch.

CHAPTER 4
POLITICAL PARTIES

INTRODUCTION

We've now reviewed the political system in the United Kingdom and taken a look at the electoral process as well. However, what we haven't spent any time on yet are political parties. That's a glaring omission, because it's impossible to fully understand the political system and the electoral process as they currently stand without taking political parties into account.

WHAT IS A POLITICAL PARTY?

Every reader will know of at least the three largest parties in United Kingdom politics: the Conservative Party (also known as the Tories); the Labour Party, and the Liberal Democrats. But what is a political party anyway?

A political party is an organisation that seeks to attain and maintain political power. They do so by putting up candidates for election in the hope of influencing the personnel and policy of the government.

Theoretically at least, a political party is made up of people who share the same ideas and will stick together, so that a vote for any of their members is a vote in favour of the party and their expressed principles and policies.

THE PARTY SYSTEM

The United Kingdom has a multiparty political system. What this means is simply that there is more than one political party which is legally allowed to hold power. The alternative to a multiparty system is a single-party system. Single-party systems are usually equated with tyranny and dictatorships. Examples of single-party systems are the current communist government in China and the Nazi government of Germany between 1933 and 1945.

While the United Kingdom is a multiparty system by design and in theory, in practice it's perhaps more correct to say that it's a 'two-party-plus' system. That is, it's a system where there are two major contenders for power of approximately equal strength, and one or more minor parties able to win seats but not form government – or at least, not without being part of a coalition.

In the United Kingdom, the Conservative Party and the Labour Party have been the two largest political parties since the 1920s. The Liberal Democrats, formed in 1988, are currently the third largest party.

POLITICAL PARTIES AND IDEOLOGY

For most of this chapter, and indeed most of this book, we'll be talking about parties as if they're just groups of people whose only common attribute is a desire to attain political power. Arguably, that's pretty accurate! However,

theoretically at least, parties differ in terms of ideology, and it's important to understand something of this before you commit to joining one.

The easiest way to explain the ideological differences between political parties is in terms of what's called the 'left-right political spectrum.' The left-right political spectrum is a common way of classifying political parties and political ideas.

Broadly speaking, parties on the Left seek to make society more egalitarian through government intervention. The mechanisms for this are a redistributive taxation system and a welfare state. If this requires larger governments and higher taxes, so be it. Parties on the Left also tend to have more liberal policies (or at least views) on social issues. This might mean being in favour of things like gay rights, the decriminalisation of drugs, secularism, and the legalisation (where currently illegal) of prostitution and abortion.

In contrast, parties that are on the Right seek to preserve traditional social orders and values. They defend private property and capitalism and usually believe more in equality of opportunity than in equality of outcome. They are suspicious of government and therefore in favour of smaller, less powerful governments. They believe in the personal responsibility of individuals and are generally against redistributive taxation and a welfare state. On social issues, parties on the Right tend to be against things such as those included on the list above.

In France, where these terms originated, the left-wing party is called 'the party of movement' and the right-wing party is called 'the party of order,' and that's a pretty helpful way to remember the distinction. Left-wing parties move with the times; right-wing parties look to maintain order.

Traditionally, the Left has included progressives, social liberals, social democrats, socialists, communists and anarchists. The Right has included conservatives, reactionaries, monarchists, nationalists and fascists.

THE MAJOR POLITICAL PARTIES OF THE UNITED KINGDOM

The discussion of political ideologies, above, raises an obvious question: where do the three major political parties of the United Kingdom sit on the political spectrum? Let's take a look.

The Labour Party

Currently the Labour Party is a centrist political party (that is, neither particularly left-wing nor particularly right-wing). However, the Labour Party was traditionally the Party of the Left in the United Kingdom and many of its members still hold left-wing beliefs. These include being in favour of the redistribution of wealth through taxation, relatively high public spending even if it means more government debt, high taxes if necessary, and protecting the rights of workers.

The Conservative Party

The Conservative Party was traditionally the Party of the Right in the United Kingdom, but like the Labour Party they currently occupy the centre ground. Still, on some issues the Conservative Party definitely leans to the right, supporting for example a 'robust' response to crime and harsher punishments for criminals.

The Liberal Democrat Party

The Liberal Democrat Party is a centre-left party. They favour redistributive taxation and the welfare state. They also advocate for electoral reform and for a reformed House of

Lords with elected members, which by rejecting tradition, can be seen as left-wing aims.

POLITICAL IDEOLOGY VS. POLITICAL PRAGMATISM

You might at this point be thinking that it's a bit strange that the three major political parties of the United Kingdom are all fairly centrist. Aren't they each meant to represent a radically different and alternative view of how things should be done?

Well yes, that is the idea! But it's politically efficacious for major parties to soften their right- or left-wing views in favour of a more centrist position most of the time. The logic works like this: voters who have strongly left-wing views are going to vote for the Party of the Left. Voters who have strongly right-wing views will vote for the Party of the Right. There's really no point in trying to appeal to these voters, as they aren't likely to be swayed. And so the only thing that makes sense is to try to appeal to uncommitted voters in the centre whose votes you might be able to attract. The only caveat is that if you go too far, you risk alienating your core vote.

This situation was brilliantly summed up by the American political scientist V. O. Key in his textbook *Politics, Parties, & Pressure Groups* (1942). He said:

> Each party leadership must maintain the loyalty of its own standpatters [NOTE: this means 'supporters']; it must also concern itself with the great blocks of voters uncommitted to either party as well as with those who may be weaned away from the opposition. These influences tend to pull the party leaderships from their contrasting anchorages toward the center. In that process, perhaps most visible in presidential campaigns, the party appeals often sound much alike and thereby contribute to the bewilderment of observers of American politics.

 how2become

Nine years later the French jurist, sociologist and politician Maurice Duverger covered the same ground but in reference to Britain in his book *Political Parties* (1951). He writes:

> Who decides whether the Conservative or the Labour party shall win the election? Not their fanatical partisans who, being unable to cast their vote for any party further to the Right or to the Left, will naturally vote for them whatever they do, but the two or three million moderate Englishmen, politically situated at the Centre, who vote sometimes Conservative, sometimes Labour. To win their votes the Conservative party is forced to attenuate its Conservatism and Labour its Socialism, both of them adopting a calm tone, a reassuring aspect. Both will have to draw up policies clearly aimed at the Centre and therefore profoundly similar.

Trying to appeal to the centre without alienating your core vote and annoying your members is of course a tricky balancing act. In many ways it's a much simpler proposition to be part of a smaller party, as smaller parties don't try to please everyone (and risk pleasing no one).

POLITICAL PARTIES AND ELECTIONS

During an election, the candidates compete with each other to win individual seats. At the same time however, political parties compete with each other for the chance to form the government.

If one party is able to win more than half the seats in the House of Commons (that is, 326 or more) then the Monarch invites the leader of that party to form a government. The leader becomes Prime Minister. All the other parties become the 'opposition.'

Actually, the strict convention is that the Prime Minister should be the member of the House of Commons who is most likely to be able to form a government with the support of that House. In practice however, this means that the leader of the political party with an absolute majority of seats in the House of Commons is chosen to be the Prime Minister.

Why is having an absolute majority important? It's because in order to pass legislation, and thereby carry out its plans, the executive needs the approval of an absolute majority of MPs in the House of Commons. By having a majority of the seats in the Commons a political party can be confident it will have enough support for its legislation during votes.

POLITICAL PARTIES IN PARLIAMENT

In an earlier chapter we said that the executive drafts prospective new laws (called bills) and introduces them into Parliament for a debate and eventually a vote on whether or not they will go onto the statute books.

In theory, MPs are able to vote entirely according to whether or not they think a proposed new law is a good idea. In practice, the MPs of the major parties are strictly controlled by party officials called whips who ensure first that they are present in Parliament for the vote, and second that they vote according to party policy. With all the MPs voting on party lines the government is very unlikely to have its proposed legislation voted down, given that they had to have a majority in order to form government in the first place.

What about the parties that are in the minority in Parliament? The minority parties and any independents form government become the opposition, but the largest of the opposition parties is given a special role to play: they become the Official Opposition (a sort of government-in-waiting) and

their leader becomes the Leader of the Opposition.

The Leader of the Opposition receives remuneration for his or her role in addition to the salary that all MPs receive. The most public function of the Leader of the Opposition is during Prime Minister's Questions. When Parliament is sitting, this is a once-weekly 30 minute session during which the Leader of the Opposition has the right to ask the Prime Minister six questions.

There's also what is called the 'Shadow Cabinet.' The Shadow Cabinet is made up of senior members of the Official Opposition. Each member of the Shadow Cabinet is given a role that mirrors that of a member of the Cabinet. Their job is to scrutinise their corresponding office holder in the government, criticise them where necessary, and develop alternative policies.

The Leader of the Opposition, the Opposition Chief Whip and Opposition Deputy Chief Whip are the only Members of the Official Opposition to draw remuneration for their Opposition roles in addition to their salaries as Members of Parliament.

SAFE VS. MARGINAL SEATS

At this point it's worth briefly considering an unofficial distinction that's nevertheless very commonly recognised in political discourse: that of 'safe' versus 'marginal' seats (seats in Parliament – that is, constituencies). These concepts are inextricably linked to political parties and to the first-past-the-post voting system that we discussed earlier as well.

Simply put, 'safe' is a label used to describe a constituency which has been secured by a particular political party. By definition, there isn't much chance of a safe seat changing hands come an election. A constituency can be safe because

of the political leanings of the electorate, because of the popularity of the incumbent, or both. Needless to say, safe seats are of huge value to political parties, as they can more or less count on winning them election after election.

In contrast, a marginal seat is one that is held by a certain party by only a small majority of votes. Marginal seats therefore require only a small swing in order to change hands. Incidentally, political parties recognise this and spend far more time and money in the lead-up to elections campaigning in marginal seats as opposed to safe ones.

To demonstrate the inertia that safe seats have, consider this: between 1955 and 1970, a period during which there were no fewer than five general elections, three quarters of the seats never changed hands. Similarly, in the three general elections between 1974 and 1979, a massive 88% of constituencies were won by the same party on all three occasions.

Of course, safe seats can and do become marginal seats and then (eventually) change hands, but it generally takes at least a few electoral cycles for this to happen. This kind of gradual shift can be associated with changing demographics of the voters in the constituency: maybe the area is attracting more retirees, more people from a particular immigrant group, or more families with young children.

More rapid changes in voter sentiment are generally associated with sudden one-off events such as the resignation, retirement or death of a popular incumbent. Having said that, genuine upsets do happen. When they do it's usually because of a strong challenge from an outside candidate such as an independent or someone from a minor party, as staunch supporters of one party are unlikely to switch and vote for 'the enemy' in the space of one electoral cycle.

It has been pointed out that the only voters with any real power to choose the government are those who live in marginal constituencies. If you live in a safe constituency then by definition your one vote won't make any difference to the outcome. And, as voting statistics tell us that less than 20% of constituencies can be considered marginal, the number of voters with the power to really influence the makeup of the House of Commons is small indeed. Some people believe that this situation is undemocratic, and would like to change it through electoral reform; a switch in voting systems from first-past-the-post to proportional representation would probably do it.

The concepts of safe and marginal seats will become highly relevant later in this book when we talk about gaining pre-selection.

CHAPTER 5
SIX STEPS TOWARDS BECOMING A POLITICIAN EDUCATION & TRAINING

Ok! Now that you've read Part I of this book you have all of the background information that you need about the political system, the electoral system, and the function and effect of political parties in the United Kingdom. It's time to move on and look at how you'll achieve your goal of becoming a politician.

Part II divides the process of becoming a politician into six steps. The first four steps, focusing on things like what you should study at university, getting relevant work experience and building a CV, are about laying the foundations, while the last two steps, dealing with preselection and with actually standing for election, are the 'pointy end' of the process.

STEP ONE: EDUCATION & TRAINING

Most careers start with education and/or training of some

kind. Chefs go to catering college. Doctors do a degree in medicine at university. Mechanics serve an apprenticeship. So if you want to become a politician, what do you study? What training do you do? How do you get the skills, experience and contacts that you'll need? Read on to find out.

School

You might be wondering why this section starts with school – aren't the things we learn at school general rather than specific?

Yes. However, there is a caveat in the case of politics. Information gathered on 620 of the 650 MPs elected at the 2010 general election shows that over one-third of them attended fee-paying schools, which is well above the United Kingdom average of just 7%. Clearly then there's some sort of correlation between attending a fee-paying school and becoming an MP.

What does this mean for you, the prospective future politician? Does it mean that if you didn't attend a fee-paying school your chances of a career in politics are shot?

Before answering that let's look at the statistics again in a little more detail, because if you do so the story gets more interesting: the percentage of the current MPs who attended a fee-paying school differs quite radically from party to party. While 54% of Conservative MPs attended a fee-paying school, the figure is 40% for Liberal Democrats and comparatively much lower at 15% for Labour MPs. So the correlation between 'attending a fee-paying school' and 'becoming an MP' is strong in the Conservative Party, still strong but a little less so for the Liberal Democrats, and not strong at all for the Labour Party (given that the percentage of people who attended fee-paying schools is almost certainly higher than average for white collar jobs in general).

What's probably happening here is that in deciding who to select as their candidates for election, the Conservatives and the Liberal Democrats consciously or unconsciously have a bias in favour of people who attended fee-paying schools. This doesn't mean you should give up if you didn't attend a fee-paying school and your goal is to become a Conservative or Liberal Democrat MP, but it is something to be aware of.

Should I go to university?
We'll talk about specific university courses much more under the next heading, but you're probably already aware that there's no university degree in 'how to be a politician.' It's not like engineering or medicine where the choice of what to study is obvious. So if that's the case, is going to university unnecessary; can you dispense with it?

Before we answer that question, it's worth pointing out that many university degrees aren't like engineering or medicine: they don't attempt to teach you specific skills for a specific job. Nevertheless, and perhaps somewhat strangely, simply having a degree (regardless of what you studied) is a requirement for many white-collar jobs.

So it appears to be with politics. How do we know this? Because 90% of the MPs elected at the 2010 general election are university graduates. That's a far, far higher percentage than you would expect if you surveyed a group of 650 people of similar ages selected at random: on average, roughly 50% of people in the United Kingdom aged between 25 and 64 have a tertiary education. Further adding to this is the fact that newly elected MPs at the 2010 general election (that is, those who had never been MPs before) were even more likely to be graduates: 94% of them had attended university.

We can say with confidence that today, people who become MPs are almost always university educated. There simply

must be something in that, and so the answer to the question in the heading is this: yes, you do need to go to university. No, you cannot dispense with it. Being an MP has effectively become a graduate profession.

Even if there wasn't such a strong correlation between university education and success in becoming an MP, there would still be another excellent reason to go to university. It's this: most degree courses significantly improve your job prospects in general. That's important, because even with hard work, natural talent and dedication to your goal, there's simply no guarantee that you will ever be able to realise your goal of becoming a politician. Too many important factors are beyond your control. Also, even if you are eventually successful, becoming a politician might take a long time. Either way, you're going to need a way to make a living, and going to university will help you do that.

What to study at university

There's no university degree in how to be a politician, and yet going to university is still a good idea. So what should you study?

All else being equal, the answer to this question is that you should study law. There are several reasons for this:

1) **Relevant knowledge.** A degree in law provides a fantastic grounding in the legal system and the legislative process. It encourages students to think about how our society is structured and how it could be different, which it is also highly relevant.

2) **Prestige and signalling.** Having studied law confers a measure of prestige on graduates, probably because it's hard to get into and because it attracts some of the brightest people. Having a law degree also signals to

others that you possess academic ability, analytical and communication skills, and the tenacity to grind your way through a demanding course of study. Both these things will open doors for you on your way to becoming a politician.

3) *Flexibility of career options.* Completing a law degree allows you to then train as a solicitor or barrister; both are generally regarded as desirable professions. If you don't want to be a lawyer, law graduates have plenty of other options, including criminology, business, human resources, international relations, journalism and education (some of these would of course require postgraduate study and/or relevant work experience). As we noted above, it's unlikely that you'll go into politics straight away, so having these options is a good thing.

Backing up these reasons is the fact that law degrees are common among politicians. A 2005 survey of MPs found that 11.7% of them came from a legal background: 5.5% of them had been barristers prior to entering politics and 6.2% of them solicitors. Many more of them would have had law degrees without being practicing lawyers: of the 645 MPs at that time, almost 400 had a degree in either law or the humanities.

So undertaking a Bachelor of Laws might be the best all-around choice if you want to become a politician. But of course, law is a competitive and demanding course of study, and difficult to get into in the first place. What if you aren't so academically inclined? In that case you should opt for a humanities degree. A degree in any of English, economics, history, political science, sociology, languages and/or philosophy would serve – really, exactly what you study

doesn't make all that much difference, so pick subjects based on what interests you and on what you'll be able to get good results in.

Of course, as we touched on above, going to university shouldn't be all about what's best for your political career. Becoming a politician is difficult, so when planning your university study it would be wise for you to think about not only what course might benefit a future political career, but also about what course will assist you in getting a job or gaining entry into a profession you might enjoy. In other words, what everyone else does when choosing a university course! So if you have a burning desire to study chemistry (... like Margaret Thatcher), go for it: you're more likely to do well at a degree you want to study, and it will be more likely to lead to a job you'll enjoy. These two outcomes are far more important than whether or not it's a 'suitable' degree for a future politician.

What university to attend

There's no denying that with tertiary education, particularly in the United Kingdom, where you study can be as important as *what* you study. So where should you study if you want to be a politician?

Again, let's examine the statistics on currently sitting MPs. First off, just fewer than three in every 10 of the current crop of MPs attended either Oxford or Cambridge. To break it down by party, 38% of Conservative MPs were educated at Oxford or Cambridge, 28% of Liberal Democrat MPs and 20% of Labour MPs.

Moving up the food chain, the proportion of 'Oxbridge' educated Ministers in the current (2010) Cabinet is very high, at 69%. This is higher than under the previous Cabinets of Labour Prime Ministers Gordon Brown (45% in 2007) and Tony Blair (16% in 1997).

As an aside, it's interesting to note that every Prime Minister since 1937 who attended university was educated at Oxford, with the sole exception of Gordon Brown.

Other universities producing high numbers of current MPs include the London School of Economics with 25, Edinburgh with 15, Manchester with 14, and Durham with 12.

So again, where should you study if you want to become a politician? Even without knowing exactly why, it seems safe to say that either Oxford or Cambridge would be the best choice if you have political ambitions. Then again, as no prospective university student in the United Kingdom would be likely to turn down an opportunity to study at one of those two universities anyway, it's a moot point. Failing an Oxbridge university, study at the best university you can, consulting the league tables if necessary and perhaps paying some special attention to the universities mentioned in the preceding paragraph.

Public speaking

There might not be a university course in how to become a politician, but there is definitely a skill set that politicians need. Chief among that skill set is the fine art of speaking before an audience.

Public speaking has of course been an essential skill for those in the political arena since ancient times. In the ancient city-state of Athens, Greece (508-322 BCE), public speaking was the most important skill someone in public life could have. Persuasive speakers were able to transcend humble origins and achieve power and influence solely due to their ability to sway an audience to their point of view. Social mobility, in other words, could be achieved with no more than some silver-tongued rhetoric.

Then again, ancient Athens didn't have Twitter, email and Facebook! Today there are multitudes of ways for a candidate or a politician to communicate with the electorate. Does that mean skill at public speaking is no longer required? No, the necessity for effective public speaking remains. Gaining preselection, for example, will almost always require that you speak in front of a group of local party members, and this is where preselection is won and lost (see Step Five: Gaining Preselection for much more on this topic).

Electronic communication methods have their place, but you have to start somewhere in connecting with people, and in person at a public event is where it will be.

If that sounds to you like a problem, the good news is that speaking is an acquired skill like any other. There's a perception that good speakers are born, not made, but don't be fooled into that way of thinking, A certain level of talent might come into it, but rest assured that every great speaker has honed their craft, speech after speech, hour after hour.

So: if you want to get better at public speaking – and if you want to become a politician, you should, no matter your current level of ability – you need to practice. Forget books, top-5-ways-to-get-better-at-public-speaking lists on the internet, YouTube videos and advice from friends. You don't learn to ride a bike that way, and you won't get better at public speaking that way either. The only way to significantly improve is to learn by doing. The organisation known as Toastmasters of Britain and Ireland has clubs literally all over the United Kingdom where you can do just that. For more information about Toastmasters check out their Wikipedia page (www.en.wikipedia.org/wiki/Toastmasters) and to find a Toastmasters club near you visit their website at: www.d71.org/portal.php.

CHAPTER 6
SIX STEPS TOWARDS
BECOMING A POLITICIAN
BUILDING A CV

STEP TWO: BUILDING A CV

No-one (well, almost no-one) becomes a politician overnight. It's a marathon, not a sprint, and you have to lay the ground-work before you'll have any chance of gaining preselection or winning an election. This chapter is devoted to teaching you how to do that.

Volunteering
All the major political parties require volunteer labour, partic-ularly at election time. Contacting the party of your choice in your local area at this time and offering to hand out leaflets, stuff envelopes or do basic office work is very likely to get a positive response.

Some parties have ways for volunteers to sign up on their main party websites. For example, the Labour Party has http://www2.labour.org.uk/volunteer.

If you find that the major parties already have all the volunteers they need, try a minor party with a candidate in the constituency where you live or someone who's standing as an independent.

Volunteering to help during an election campaign offers you some great opportunities. One is gaining an intimate knowledge of the process; seeing how a campaign is run. You'll learn the issues that voters take seriously and want a candidate to address. Another opportunity is getting to know the candidate you're volunteering for personally and seeing how they work professionally as well.

Also, and crucially, the candidates (not just the one you're working for) will learn who you are. Especially if you volunteer a couple of times, your name will become familiar to local party members.

While the work that you do might be menial, simply having the experience on your CV will also give you a useful edge over your competition in applying, for example, for an internship.

Perhaps best of all, if you make yourself useful to a candidate who goes on to win his or her seat, you might very well find that you have gained a highly useful friend and contact who's a Westminster insider.

INTERNSHIPS - Part I
You probably already know what an internship is, but just in case, here's a refresher: an intern is someone who works in a temporary position with an emphasis on on-the-job training rather than merely employment. Interns get the opportunity to gain experience in a certain field, see if they have an interest in a particular career, and create a network of contacts. In return, employers get cheap or free labour, though usually just for low-level tasks.

Internships are common in politics, both here and in other countries. Completing an internship in Westminster or with a relevant organisation such as a think tank will give your political ambitions a massive boost. First and foremost, an internship offers the opportunity to make contacts, which could be vital in gaining preselection (see Step Five, later on in this book, for much more on this topic). An internship will also allow you to get experience which could lead to a paying job in politics, which would provide an even better opportunity to make contacts and build a profile within a party.

Internships are usually done at the 'life stage' where you're still at university or have just graduated, but in fact there's nothing to stop you from applying for one no matter where you're at.

Getting an internship is, of course, not easy. It's a buyer's market with many applicants for every vacancy. The best places with MPs, think tanks and other political bodies are fiercely contested.

But how do you find a placement in the first place? Here are the main two ways:

1) *Mass-mail your CV to MPs, think tanks and other relevant organisations on a speculative basis.*

The 'shotgun' approach. If you're wondering where to find addresses, contact details for all the sitting MPs can be found on the www.parliament.uk website, and you can find a list of think tanks in the United Kingdom on Wikipedia (do a search at www.wikipedia.org for 'UK think tanks').

This approach is of course low on effort. The downside is that unless you tailor your cover letter extremely well and have a very impressive CV it's likely to get ignored. For best results, research your targets carefully. For example, research individual MPs on the www.parliament.uk website

and elsewhere and then tailor your application to what you find out about them. Start with MPs who you have something in common with (perhaps you went to the same school) and emphasise this connection, or mention that you agree with a particular policy stance of theirs (be sincere where possible!).

2)   *Look for advertised listings.*

One of the best places to find advertisements for relevant internships is the Work for an MP website (www.w4mp.org). It lists advertisements for internships (and in fact, paying jobs) with MPs, think tanks, government departments and non-government organisations. There are also listings at the Electus Start website (www.electus-start.com) along with advice about how to get a job in politics. Lastly, you can try the 'jobs' sections on the websites of the major parties. They are www.labour.org.uk/jobs (Labour), www.conservatives.com/Get_involved/Jobs.aspx (the Conservatives) and www.libdems.org.uk/jobs.aspx (the Liberal Democrats).

Any advertised internship is of course going to attract a lot of applications, so yours will need to stand out. Keep your CV succinct and no more than two pages with a normal font size (10-12 pt). Highlight things such as any volunteer work in politics that you've done, involvement with your Student Union, having written for the student newspaper at your university, being a member of a debating society and so on. Ideally your CV and cover letter will provide a convincing narrative of how you got to the point of wanting to work for an MP.

Whichever method you adopt, be persistent: the numbers are stacked against you, so it may take some time before you're successful. Keep in mind that while it might be the ideal op-

tion, a relevant internship need not be in Westminster. Consider also internships in Europe, for example in Brussels. The European jobsite EuroBrussels (www.eurobrussels.com) is a good place to look for these opportunities.

INTERNSHIPS - Part II

So you've been lucky/good enough to secure an internship, let's assume in Westminster with an MP. Is everything rosy? Unfortunately not. Finding an internship opportunity is in fact only half the battle. Once you start your internship you're going to encounter a couple of big problems. They are: 1) you don't get paid, and 2) you have to live in London while you're not getting paid.

Across the parties only 1% of MPs pay their interns, and even then it's only the minimum wage. Expenses such as travel and food are meant to be covered, but often the allowance given (£5 a day is common) isn't even enough for that. Worse still, doing an internship means that you surrender your right to benefits. Jobseekers' Allowance does not pay out if you are undertaking work experience.

Given that supporting yourself in London costs around £2000 for a three month period at current (2010) rates, and that internships are generally full-time, you'll need to work out what you're going to do for money. If you can stay for free with friends or family who live in London that will of course help to reduce your costs. You might be able to manage a part-time job (working nights and weekends) alongside an internship, but it'll be very tough, particularly if you have to travel a significant distance to get to your internship from where you live.

Unfortunately, many interns are forced to exhaust their savings, rely on student loans and grants, or use overdrafts and credit cards in order to complete their internship. A lucky few

are of course able to rely on parental support.

If money is going to be an issue for you, and if you're still at university, consider doing an internship during university holidays as opposed to after you graduate. That way you'll have the financial support of your student loan to look forward to when you start term again. If you do an internship after you graduate you'll have no such guarantee, as for most people an internship doesn't lead immediately to a paying job.

Incidentally, there are a lot of people calling for Westminster interns to be paid at least the minimum wage rather than having to work for free. The feeling is that at the moment, the majority of Westminster internship opportunities are limited to those whose parents can support them. 'Intern Aware' for example, is a campaign focusing on promoting fairer access to the internship system (www.internaware.org). You might want to keep an eye on this debate.

For general 'inside information' on doing an internship, a great source is the website/blog Interns Anonymous (www. internsanonymous.co.uk).

Paid Jobs in Politics

After volunteering and completing an internship, the next logical step is a paying job in politics. The archetypal paid job in politics is working as a politician's assistant, so that's what we'll focus on in this section.

You might wonder why this section doesn't appear below in Step 2: Work Prior to Entering Politics. The reason is that you don't work as a politician's assistant because that's what you want to do with your life. You work as a politician's assistant because you want to become politician yourself. As such it's definitely a CV-building activity.

So what do politicians' assistants do? Broadly, they provide

administrative, secretarial, research, constituency, parliamentary and publicity support to MPs. The actual job title of a politicians' assistant may be variously: parliamentary assistant (or constituency assistant, depending on where the job is based); personal assistant; research assistant; case worker, or executive secretary. Job titles and locations vary, but the basic task is to do whatever behind-the-scenes work is necessary to enable MPs to represent their constituents. Each MP typically has between one and three assistants.

Here's a list of specific duties that an assistant to a politician might be required to perform:

- Respond to enquiries from constituents, other politicians, the media, lobbyists and pressure groups;

- Progress casework from constituent enquiries;

- Secretarial duties, such as managing the politician's diary, making travel arrangements and taking minutes at meetings;

- Undertake administrative duties, such as updating databases, filing, ordering stationery and responding to correspondence;

- Carry out research into local, regional, national and international issues and ensure the politician is made aware of any relevant matters;

- Develop knowledge on specialist areas;

- Arrange surgeries and offer support on the day;

- Write press releases, newsletters and 'mailshots' to promote the work of the politician and keep constituents and interested parties informed;

- Monitor and arrange media coverage;

- Assist with campaigns before and during elections;

- Keep up to date with current affairs;

- Attend public and private functions to assist the politician and stand in when the politician is unable to attend;

- Liaise with members of government and local government, party head quarters, other politicians and their staff, embassies, commissioners, relevant interest groups, the media, relevant voluntary sector organisations and constituents;

- Help write speeches by researching information and making suggestions on content;

- Help draft amendments for reports;

- Prepare briefing material;

- Provide the politician with the support needed to get an issue on the political agenda, for example research or liaising with key individuals or groups;

- Update the politician's website, and

- Manage other paid staff within the constituency or parliamentary office, including interns, volunteers and work placement.

As you can see, this is a highly demanding job; the list of duties is daunting. However, it's also absolutely unbeatable experience and the chance to make contacts is unmatched.

To find a job as a politician's assistant again the first place to look should be the Work for an MP website (www.w4mp. org). Apply as you would for any other job, highlighting any volunteer work or internships you have completed in the political sphere.

Student Politics

If you're currently a university student, or will be in the future, another CV building opportunity presents itself in the form of with student politics. There are three reasons:

1) ***Experience.*** The process of giving speeches, campaigning, trying to get elected, and working with others to make decisions when in power is broadly the same whether you're dealing with national debt or the price of beer in the student union. The stakes are low, making it invaluable risk-free practice for the real thing.

2) ***Pure CV building.*** The second reason to enter student politics is so that you can say you've done it. You're more likely to be able to impress a major political party of your bona fides, and therefore gain preselection, if you can point to a successful stint in student politics.

3) ***Making contacts.*** Some student politicians go on to become 'real' politicians after they graduate from university. That should be obvious; it's what you want to do! Getting involved with student politics gives you the opportunity to meet fellow student politicians, any of whom might enter 'real' politics one day. If one of them does so before you do, then you've potentially gained a contact who can give you advice and assistance in following the same path.

Just like for 'real' politics, the easiest way into student politics is to volunteer to help out at election time. And/or you can join the main parties' political clubs and get involved that way – an added bonus is that at larger universities they tend to get good invited speakers you might be able to meet.

Local Politics

Earlier in this book we touched on the different levels of gov-

ernment and noted that there are a total of 433 local authorities in the United Kingdom. We also noted that those local authorities are run by councils, and that the councillors are elected. So might running to be a councillor a good apprenticeship and CV building opportunity before a tilt at becoming an MP?

It might be. It's certainly not unheard of for people in local government to step up to Central Government at some stage, and it's definitely a great way of getting to be well-known in a constituency. For example, the current Liberal Democrat MP for Lewes, Norman Baker, was leader of Lewes District Council before he stood in and won a general election.

It might be that this approach is better suited to members of the Liberal Democrats however, as their support tends to be more localised – the Liberal Democrats traditionally poll well in areas where they have a strong local party with representation on councils. This is less true of the Conservatives and the Labour Party.

Unfortunately, it's beyond the scope of this book to go into a detailed examination of how to get into local government. However, most of the advice and principles espoused here apply just as well to becoming a local government councillor as they do to becoming an MP. For further information, go first of all to the Communities and Local Government website, where there is a page devoted to the subject of 'How to become a Councillor' (www.communities.gov.uk/local-government/about/councillor). Then check the websites of councils in your area for the specifics.

General CV Building

In this chapter we've looked at five avenues for adding marquee entries to your CV. All well and good, but there are plenty of other, less obvious opportunities for adding things

to your CV that will play very well went you want to gain pre-selection and even get elected.

In particular, you should actively seek out *anything that shows you have a commitment to public service.* This often translates into unpaid work for the benefit of your local community. For example, you could: coach a kid's football team; help a local charity out with free labour; get involved with fundraising for a local school or club or charity; serve on the board of a local community organisation, and even set up your own local community organisation for the benefit of a needy group or to provide a needed service.

It's best if these activities come out of your own particular skills, interests, hobbies, contacts and knowledge – but if you're stuck for an idea, the internet can help. Try first of all the Directgov website (go to www.direct.gov.uk and do a search for 'volunteering').

CHAPTER 7
SIX STEPS TOWARDS BECOMING A POLITICIAN: WORK PRIOR TO ENTERING POLITICS

STEP THREE: WORK PRIOR TO ENTERING POLITICS

There are definitely some 'career politicians' who get involved with student politics, go on to work as an assistant to a politician after graduation, then become a candidate, and finally become an MP. David Cameron is a prime example (see his short biography in the Appendix of this book).

Despite some criticism of this route into politics – many people think politicians should have experience in the 'real world,' whatever that means – from a purely selfish perspective it's definitely the best way to go, and for that reason it's what this book focuses on helping you to do.

On the other hand, no-one should bank on the career politician route working out. You don't actually become a

politician until you win an election, and there's no telling when (or indeed, if) that will happen. Also, elections only come around every so often, and standing for election is expensive. No, unless you're independently wealthy, you're going to need a job. But what job?

What Do Most Politicians Do?

We've already seen that the overwhelming majority of MPs are university graduates, and that they have usually studied law or the humanities. So what do most future MPs do before they become MPs?

The following table, which is available in the public domain at www.parliament.uk, is instructive:

MPS' Occupations 1987 to 2005

% of all from main parties (Conservative/Labour/Liberal Democrat)

	#					%				
	1987	1992	1997	2001	2005	1987	1992	1997	2001	2005
PROFESSIONS	262	258	272	270	242	41.7	41.1	43.2	42.9	39.3
Barrister	57	53	36	33	34	9.1	8.5	5.7	5.2	5.5
Solicitor	31	30	28	35	38	4.9	4.8	4.5	5.6	6.2
Doctor	5	6	9	8	6	.8	1.0	1.4	1.3	1.0
Civil Service/local govt	22	26	37	35	28	3.5	4.1	5.9	5.6	4.6
Teachers: University/college	36	45	61	53	44	5.7	7.2	9.7	8.4	7.2
Teacher: School	48	57	65	64	47	7.6	9.1	10.3	10.2	7.6
BUSINESS	161	152	113	107	118	25.6	24.2	18.0	17.0	19.2
MISCELLANEOUS	133	154	188	200	217	21.1	24.6	29.9	31.7	35.3
White Collar	27	46	72	76	78	4.3	7.3	11.4	12.1	12.7
Politician/Pol organiser	34	46	60	66	87	5.4	7.3	9.5	10.5	14.1
Publisher/Journalist	42	44	47	50	43	6.7	7.0	7.5	7.9	7.0
MANUAL WORKERS	73	63	56	53	39	11.6	10.0	8.9	8.4	6.2
Miners	17	13	13	12	11	2.7	2.1	2.1	1.9	1.8
TOTAL	629	627	629	630	615	100	100	100	100	100

Source: Butler et al The British General Election of 2005 and earlier editions

This gives a helpful picture of what MPs do prior to becoming MPs, albeit with some obvious limitations: the second-largest category, Business, doesn't tell us much, and the sub-category White Collar under Miscellaneous is similarly unhelpful. These labels could mean just about anything.

Still, we can see that as expected, lawyers have made up a decent percentage of MPs in each of the five surveyed years, ranging from a high of 14% of the MPs from the three major parties in 1987 to a low of 10.2% in 1997.

The lawyers may be expected, but what is more surprising is the high numbers of teachers. In 1997 fully 20% of the MPs from the three major parties were either school or university teachers. Having said that, the figure has declined since then and in 2005 was lower at 14.8%. Still, that's a significant percentage. It's perhaps in keeping with the fact that many would-be MPs complete humanities degrees, which lead naturally to teaching jobs.

The most striking set of figures in this table is the row for Politician/Political organiser. From 1987 to 2005 they go 34 – 46 – 60 – 66 – 87, and the last figure represents 14.1% of the MPs from the three major parties. That is undoubtedly due to the rise of the 'career politician,' and it shows the efficacy of that route into Parliament. One suspects that the figure would have jumped again following the 2010 general election (figures are not available yet).

Finally, we can also see the percentage of manual workers steadily declines, lending strength to the statement expressed earlier in this book that being an MP has become a graduate profession.

What's the ideal job for a would-be politician?
Let's set aside for now what most future MPs actually do

before they become MPs and think about the theoretical 'ideal job' for a would-be politician. What characteristics are important? Here are some:

1) **Flexibility.** Ideally, you want a job with enough flexibility that you can put it on hold or scale it back while pursuing elected office. You don't want a job that will trap you into long term obligations that'll be hard to get out of when the time is right for you to stand for election. Working for yourself is definitely an advantage here.

2) **At least reasonable pay.** We'll see that standing for election is costly, and one way or another you're likely to spend quite a bit of your own money, even if it's just supporting yourself while you run. It would be nice if your job was well paid enough that you could save some money before running, and well paid enough that you could get back on your feet reasonably quickly if you don't win.

3) **Contact with people.** It's a big plus if your job brings you into contact with a lot of local people. Why? Because meeting and dealing with people in your working life can't fail to put you in touch with the concerns that people have (invaluable for a would-be MP), not to mention it'll help you build your communication skills. Jobs and professions which allow you to meet a lot of local people day-to-day include lawyer, doctor, small business owner, journalist and teacher, though this is by no means an exhaustive list.

(Also, in the event that you end up standing for election in the constituency where you live, already knowing a lot of local people and having their support will give your election campaign a huge head-start.)

4) ***Something you could return to relatively easily.***
Politics is an inherently unstable career choice, and
even if you succeed in winning a seat there's no
guarantee you won't lose it again after an election
or two. Such is life! Consequently you might be very
thankful for a job or career you can slip back into
relatively easily after a break lasting four years,
eight years or longer.

5) ***Something you enjoy.*** Finally, an 'ideal job' has of
course to be something that you enjoy doing. As we
noted in Step One: Education & Training, your political
dreams may never become reality, or may take a long
time to realise. It would therefore be a mistake to plan
your working life on the basis that it'll only be a few
years before you become an MP. Just like everyone
else, you need to find work that you'd be happy (or
perhaps more realistically, not too unhappy) to do, if
necessary, for a long time.

So what job meets all of those criteria? Well, criteria **5)** is
obviously an individual thing, but leaving that aside, let's take
the short list in criteria **3)** – lawyer, doctor, small business
owner, journalist and teacher – and see if the other criteria
knock any of them out.

Because journalism is so focused on current events and
trends, and constantly moves with the times, it's not a job
you can easily return to, so that rules it out on the basis
of criteria **4)**. Medicine is questionable for the same reason,
and it's also not a flexible profession, so let's rule out doctor.
Teaching may be marginal in terms of criteria **2)**, pay, but at
least there's always plenty of demand for teachers, which
means less time out of work, so we'll leave it in.

So our short list then is lawyer, small business owner and teacher. These three jobs meet the first four criteria; it's up to you to say whether they fail or succeed on criteria **5)**. That short list looks pretty good/accurate given that in 2005 they together represented the occupations of 33.5% of the sitting MPs of the three major parties (see table above).

Of course, there are probably many other jobs that would meet our first four criteria (though criteria **3)** can be tricky). They are mostly to be found in the 'white collar' world, either in civil service or in private enterprise; you'll need to make your own assessment on these on a case-by-case basis.

CHAPTER 8
SIX STEPS TOWARDS
BECOMING A POLITICIAN
JOINING A POLITICAL PARTY

STEP FOUR: JOINING A POLITICAL PARTY

Earlier in this book we explored the nature and the role of political parties in the modern United Kingdom. In this section we're going to look at the role they will play in helping you to get elected.

Why Join a Political Party?
We know what political parties are. But why would you want to join one?

The answer is very straightforward, and is illustrated by the following fact: of the 646 MPs sitting immediately prior to the 2010 general election, all but one belonged to a political party. That proportion (645 to 1) is so overwhelming

that it would be fair to say that for all practical purposes, it is impossible to become an MP unless you belong to a political party. Forget about standing as an independent: it's a complete waste of time.

But why do members of political parties hold such a huge advantage when it comes to getting elected? There are two reasons. First, as a party member you have in your corner a well-funded, highly experienced organisation whose goal is to ensure that all its candidates succeed in getting elected. Second, as a party member people will vote for you simply because they want your party to form government, regardless what they think of you or even whether they think about you at all.

YOU NEED TO JOIN A PARTY. BUT WHICH ONE?

What party to join

Our earlier chapter on political parties focused exclusively on the 'big three': the Conservatives, Labour and the Liberal Democrats. So far, we haven't discussed any of the smaller parties, and you might be wondering why not. Mightn't it be easier to gain preselection with a smaller party where there's less competition?

Probably. But leaving that aside for a moment, here's a list of some of the smaller political parties in the United Kingdom. These are the parties that currently (following the 2010 general election) have at least one seat in the House of Commons (excluding of course the 'big three'):

- ***The Democratic Unionist Party.*** This is a hard-line Unionist party from Northern Ireland. The Democratic Unionist Party is right-wing on social issues but (at least historically) centre-left on economic issues. They have

many seats in the Northern Ireland Assembly but only eight in the House of Commons.

- ***The Scottish National Party.*** This is a centre-left party whose goal is Scottish independence. The Scottish National Party has six seats in the House of Commons.

- ***Sinn Féin.*** Sinn Féin is the Irish Republican party in Northern Ireland – they want an Irish republic free from British involvement. They have five seats in the House of Commons.

- ***Plaid Cymru (Party of Wales).*** Yet another party in favour of independence, this one from Wales. Currently Plaid Cymru has three Seats in the House of Commons.

- ***The Social Democratic and Labour Party.*** This Irish nationalist party is centre-left and social democratic. Three seats in the House of Commons (16 in Ireland).

- ***The Alliance Party of Northern Ireland.*** This party aims to breakdown sectarian divisions between Catholics and Protestants in Northern Ireland. It has a neutral stance on the issue of Northern Ireland's status. The Alliance Party of Northern Ireland is linked with the Liberal Democrats. One seat in the House of Commons.

- ***Green Party of England and Wales.*** A relatively new party focused, of course, on environmental issues. One seat in the House of Commons.

Do you see some problems here? Four of these parties are based in Northern Ireland. Unless you're from Northern Ireland and share a very specific set of political beliefs with one of them, you can forget about those four. Of the others, one is Scottish and one is Welsh. Again, unless you're from (respectively) Scotland or Wales and a passionate supporter of Scottish or Welsh independence, they're no good to you.

So who does that leave? It leaves the Green Party of England and Wales, proud holders of...a single seat in the House of Commons.

Hopefully this makes the answer to the question at the top of this section clear: you should disregard the smaller parties completely and join the Conservatives, Labour or the Liberal Democrats. It doesn't matter if it's easier to gain preselection for a smaller party if doing so provides you with no significantly greater chance of getting elected than if you stood as an independent.

Why are the Major Parties so Dominant?

After reading the previous section you might be wondering why there aren't more centrist, multi-issue parties with significant numbers of seats in Westminster.

Remember our discussion on electoral systems in an earlier chapter? The fact that we use the first-past-the-post electoral system for general elections in the United Kingdom means that the dominance of the two major parties (that is, Labour and the Conservatives) is favoured and maintained. A smaller party could poll well; coming second or third in many constituencies and thereby getting a large percentage of the popular vote across the country, but still not win any (or many) seats. This in fact happened in the 2005 general election, when the Liberal Democrat party took more than a fifth of the total votes but only about a tenth of the seats (62) in Parliament.

It's true that at the last general election the Liberal Democrats significantly increased their number of seats in the House of Commons, and were even invited to form half of a coalition government, but for now the United Kingdom is still a 'two-party-plus' system as was discussed earlier. The Conservatives and Labour are major contenders for power

of approximately equal strength, and the Liberal Democrats are able to win seats but remain very unlikely to be able to form government on their own any time soon.

It's possible that in the future the United Kingdom will adopt some other electoral system that's better able to reflect diversity in the electorate's voting preferences. For now however, it's first-past-the-post, and for you that means if you want to get elected, you need to throw your hat in the ring with one of the three major parties.

Are There Any Negatives to Joining a Political Party?

We've already said that joining a political party is essential if you want to become a politician. Ok, so it might be unavoidable. But nonetheless are there downsides to living your life your political life as a member of a party?

Yes, but only once you've been elected. The largest downside to being a party member as an MP is that you lose almost all of your free will. As we noted earlier, MPs that belong to the major parties are strictly controlled by party officials known as whips. The whips try to ensure that party members vote according to party policy, and they almost always succeed in this because not toeing the party line could get you expelled from the party. That means you have no option but to vote the way you're told to rather than in the way you might prefer. If you want to become a politician because you have strong ideas and opinions that you want to follow through on, then having to do what you're told could present a problem.

On the other hand, the alternative to joining a political party – standing as an independent – is no better. Even if you're able to get elected, your one vote in a House with 650 Members is going to make absolutely no difference to anything, except in the highly unlikely scenario that the number of seats held by the major parties is so nearly equal that courting your vote becomes important.

So: the choice boils down to being constrained or being ineffectual. Constrained is definitely the better option!

How to Join a Political Party

Joining a political party is usually as simple as choosing to do so, filling out a form and perhaps paying a nominal fee. Do this and congratulations, you're a member! However, being a rank-and-file member of a political party doesn't mean all that much. The real battles are getting a profile within the party and gaining preselection (which we'll deal with at length in the next chapter).

When to Join

This may be Step Four in our six-step series, but in fact there's no reason not to join a political party as soon as you're sure which one you favour. After all, the sooner you're a party member the sooner you can start to get noticed within the party.

If you're still young, you can join the youth wing of one of the three major parties. Here are their details:

- For the youth wing of the Conservative Party go to:
  www.conservativefuture.com

- For the Liberal Democrats youth site go to:
  www.liberalyouth.org

- For the Young Labour website go to:
  www.labour.org.uk/younglabour

Otherwise, just join as an ordinary adult member. You'll find details of how to do so on the main websites:

- The main Conservative Party website is at:
  www.conservatives.com

- The main Liberal Democrats website is at:
  www.libdems.org.uk

- The main Labour Party website is at:
  www2.labour.org.uk/home

Once you've joined, look out for events near you that you can attend.

For the Labour Party, you can sign up to be notified of events near you at: www2.labour.org.uk/events_near_me.

You can also try the new 'Membersnet' tool at: www.members.labour.org.uk/my-membership-details.

For the Liberal Democrats, check out the website Liberal Democrats Flock Together (www.flocktogether.org.uk).

For the Conservative Party, try the 'Find your local conservative' on the front page of their website at: www.conservatives.com.

CHAPTER 9
SIX STEPS TOWARDS BECOMING A POLITICIAN: GAINING PRESELECTION

STEP FIVE: GAINING PRESELECTION

Preselection is the process by which a candidate is selected by a political party to contest an election for political office. It's without a doubt the most important step on the path to becoming a politician.

In this chapter we'll look at why preselection is so important, how the major parties pick their candidates, and what you need to do in order to be one of the people that they pick.

NOTE: Preselection is also referred to as 'candidate selection,' and in fact this nomenclature is more common in the United Kingdom. However, 'preselection' is a clearer, less ambiguous term, which is why it is used throughout this book.

Why is Preselection so Important?
In the last chapter we said that members of political parties

hold a huge advantage when it comes to getting elected. That's true, but it's not the whole truth: in fact, what counts is not just being a member of a political party – anyone can do that – it's getting endorsed by the party you belong to as the candidate who will contest a particular seat on behalf of the party. Being able to stand as an endorsed candidate of a major party is what counts, and that's why preselection is so critical.

How do the major parties choose candidates?

The three major parties choose their candidates in much the same way, with a two-stage process. The first stage involves being assessed by the party's central office. Get through this stage and your name will be added to an approved list of suitable candidates. The second stage involves being assessed by local party members within an individual constituency.

In the next section we'll look at the first stage of this process in detail, using specifically the Conservative Party's preselection process as an example.

PRESELECTION STAGE I

The Conservative Party's approved list of candidates is kept by the Candidates Department in Conservative Campaign Headquarters (formerly known as Conservative Central Office), located at 30 Millbank, Westminster. If you want to get on this list, the first step is simply to send an application and a CV to Conservative Campaign Headquarters.

Conservative Campaign Headquarters considers all the applications it receives and recommends some of them for consideration by a Parliamentary Assessment Board. This is a day-long assessment by current Conservative MPs and

senior Party volunteers. There's a £250 fee for attending a Parliamentary Assessment Board and you must have been a member of the Party for at least 3 months before you can attend one.

Candidates who are successful at the Parliamentary Assessment Board stage have their names added to the approved list, subject to final approval by staff from the Candidates Department and some MPs.

Now the Local Conservative Associations in the various constituencies come into play. Sitting MPs are normally reselected automatically if they want to run again, but if there is a vacancy for a candidate at election time, the association will inform Campaign Headquarters. Campaign Headquarters will then tell all of the candidates on the approved list that the constituency is looking to select a candidate, and those wishing to apply send their CVs directly to the Local Conservative Association in that con-stituency for consideration.

How do you get approved at Stage I?
What do you need to have on your CV to get a 'foot in the door' at Stage I? Well, unsurprisingly, the better known you are in your party, the better your chances of avoiding the reject pile. This is why volunteering, doing an internship and working as an assistant for an MP are such effective ways of furthering your political ambitions.

Aside from that, things you should highlight in your CV and cover letter include:

- Work you've done for the good of your local community, particularly unpaid work;

- Achievements in your work or personal life which show that you would make an effective MP (how you argue this

is up to you, be creative!);

• Any leadership roles that you have or have had; and

• In general, anything that shows you have a commitment to public service.

Remember, what parties want above all are candidates that they think can win, so do your best to emphasise your electability.

Seeking preselection in your area vs. seeking it elsewhere

Having dealt with Stage I of the preselection process, let's now assume that you're on the approved list with a major party and consequently you'll be informed of any constituencies that need a candidate when there's an impending election.

Before we go on to consider Stage II of the preselection process, it's worth digressing to consider two important questions. First, can you seek to stand for election in an area other than the one you live in? And second, should you?

The answer to the first question is, of course, yes. As we've seen from our examination of Stage I of the preselection process, once you're on the approved list there's nothing to prevent you from applying for preselection in any constituency that announces a vacancy.

The answer to the second is also an emphatic yes. There's a hefty advantage in being a local when applying for preselection. The reason for this is pretty obvious and intuitive: people generally have more faith in a local person to understand them and to represent them conscientiously than they would in an 'outsider.' This faith translates into more votes on polling day. The party members who do the candidate selection at the constituency level recognise this bias, and it makes them more likely to pick you over

an outsider if you're a local as they want a candidate with the best chance of winning. Besides which, as local people themselves, they'd also prefer a local to represent them, just like the rest of the electorate.

Finally, preselection aside, those 'more votes on polling day' are of course also a good thing for you.

Basically, it is in any would-be politician's interests to prioritise seeking preselection in the area where they live – or perhaps where they grew up – as opposed to any other.

The problem, of course, is that while there are 650 constituencies in the United Kingdom, there's only one that you live in, and maybe one more that you grew up in, and any one constituency might be an unsuitable location for your tilt at becoming a politician for all sorts of reasons. First, it might be a safe seat for the other party. Second, there might be no vacancy for a candidate. And third, you might apply for preselection there but fail, even with your local advantage.

Really, unless you're very lucky, you're going to have to apply for preselection in constituencies other than ones where you can claim to be a local.

Happily, non-locals gain preselection for seats all the time. Margaret Thatcher, for example, wasn't a local when she was selected as the Conservative candidate for Finchley in 1959. 'Finchley was not an area of London that I knew particularly well,' she wrote in her memoirs. She went on to become the MP for Finchley at the next election, a position she held for three decades.

If you're seeking preselection in an area where you're not a local though, it's important to take some steps to mitigate the fact that you're an outsider. More on this below.

PRESELECTION STAGE II

The second stage of the preselection process is the one where the local party organisations have all the power. Again we'll use the Conservative Party's process as an example; the other major parties use a very similar process.

Having announced a vacancy for a candidate, the Local Conservative Association receives a stack of applications from candidates on the approved list. The Association's executive goes through the CVs and chooses some to invite for an interview, which is conducted by members of the Association.

Following the interviews, a shortlist of between three and five hopefuls is compiled. Then there's a selection meeting which is open to every member of the Local Association to attend. All the candidates speak and are then subject to questioning by the members. At the end of the selection meeting all the members are entitled to vote and the person with the majority of the votes is formally adopted as the candidate for that constituency.

How do you get approved at Stage II?

We've talked about how to get the approval of your party's central office. But how about the local party members? Here's a short list of qualities that they generally look for:

- Campaigning experience;
- Knowledge of the party at local and national level, and
- A background within the party.

Hopefully at the point where you're applying for preselection you already have (and can show) these three things in abundance.

Aside from these qualities however, it's important that you also do what you can to demonstrate some respect for the

area where you're applying for preselection (we're assuming here that you're not a local). You don't have to be able to point to three generations of your family in the local church graveyard but you have to convince people of your ability to empathise with them and understand their specific needs.

To do this, you should first of all ensure that you have a good picture of the demographics, the economy, the significant institutions and the problems of their area. This isn't hard to attain: all you need to do is read the local newspapers and talk to some local people (try a pub!). If possible, try to draw a link between the issues facing the constituency and the issues in the area where you grew up, or where you're living now – it's quite possible that there are similarities even if the two places are geographically distant.

Also, try to show a connection, no matter how trivial, with the area. Perhaps you have friends or family in the constituency or you can relate an anecdote about some time you spent there. Maybe the place where you grew up is a similar size, or has similar demographics or a similar main industry, so that you can draw a link between them.

Finally, emphasise the commitment that you would have to the area if you were selected. Say that if you became the MP for the area you would of course make the commitment of moving into the constituency and immersing yourself in the community. Also say that you would select a team of locals for your constituency office.

It's all in the seat (safe and marginal seats revisited)
In an earlier chapter we discussed the concepts of safe and marginal seats. We noted that safe seats are of immense value to political parties and that parties spend much more of their time and money campaigning (or more correctly, helping their candidate to campaign) in winnable marginal seats.

 how2become

Now that we're focusing on preselection, the distinction between safe and marginal seats becomes crucial. Obviously, what you want (what any would-be politician wants) is to gain preselection for a safe seat. That way, theoretically at least, you're guaranteed of winning the seat. For this reason, preselection for a party's safe seats is usually fiercely contested, although challenges to the nomination of sitting members is usually restricted or forbidden.

Parties will usually try to ensure that their most senior, most talented members stand for election in one of their safe seats. That way, those politicians can stay in Parliament and focus on ministerial roles for long periods without the distraction of having to campaign hard or focus on electorate-specific issues at election time.

Needless to say, as a first-time candidate there is zero chance that your party will allow you to stand for election in one of their safe seats. If you're preselected at all, it's much more likely to be for a constituency that's safe for another party. That way your party risks nothing: if you lose it was expected anyway, and in the unlikely event that you win, the party gains a seat in Parliament.

So what's the point getting preselected for a seat that you have almost no chance of winning? Actually, plenty. Running in an unwinnable seat is the perfect opportunity for a would-be politician to gain experience and get more of a profile within their party. Make some good speeches, campaign hard, take some votes from the incumbent, and there's every chance that next election you'll find it much easier to gain preselection for a more winnable seat.

Need convincing of the efficacy of this route into Parliament? Go to Appendix I of this book and count how many of our last five Prime Ministers took exactly this path into power.

CHAPTER 10
SIX STEPS TOWARDS BECOMING A POLITICIAN: STANDING FOR ELECTION

STEP SIX: STANDING FOR ELECTION

How do you get a job? For just about any job, you first need to apply. Then you'll need to send in a CV, have one or more interviews, perhaps sit a test, give references and maybe even appear before a selection panel. And for politics? To become a politician it's much easier: you just need to stand for election!

Who can stand for election, and how you do it, are things that are governed by law. Unfortunately, but perhaps predictably, it's a somewhat complicated process. Accordingly, this chapter is divided into two parts. The first part deals with the nuts and bolts of standing for election; the second deals with campaigning for votes.

PROCEDURES, PREREQUISITES AND MORE

The right to stand for election is not totally unrestricted. In order to be allowed to stand, you must first of all be over 18 years of age. Second, a prospective candidate must be either a British citizen, a citizen of a Commonwealth country with indefinite leave to remain in the United Kingdom, or a citizen of the Republic of Ireland. Third, you can't be an MP (and therefore can't stand for election) if you're a civil servant, an undischarged bankrupt, a member of the clergy, police or armed forces, or a prisoner serving more than a year in jail. You also can't stand for election if you've been found guilty in the past of certain electoral offences.

Hopefully none of that should be a problem! If you pass the requirements then you can become a candidate just by saying that you are from the moment that Parliament is dissolved. However, in order for your name to appear on the ballot paper on polling day (and let's face it, this is the important bit), you have to become what's called a 'validly nominated' candidate.

Becoming validly nominated

To become validly nominated you must complete a set of nomination forms and submit them to a person called the Returning Officer. The Returning Officer is the person who is responsible for the administration of the election in your constituency. (Actually, in England and Wales, the post of Returning Officer is an honorary one, and in practice the job is delegated to an Acting Returning Officer).

In order to find out who the (Acting) Returning Officer in your constituency is and how to contact him or her, you'll need to get in touch with your local United Kingdom Electoral Commission Office. You'll find contact details for the various

local offices located in Appendix III of this book.

Nomination forms

You can get hold of the nomination forms from the (Acting) Returning Officer in your constituency, or alternatively they're available on the Electoral Commission website (www. electoralcommission.org.uk) in .pdf format.

The nomination forms that you need to get, fill out and submit are detailed below:

A Nomination Paper

The nomination paper is the key nomination form. It's pretty simple – it just asks for your name and the names and signatures of 10 registered electors from the constituency. These 10 electors are known as subscribers, and the first two subscribers are known as the proposer and seconder.

You should check that your subscribers definitely are registered electors (don't take their word for it) using a copy of the electoral register. Once you become a candidate you will be entitled to a free copy of the electoral register from an Electoral Registration Officer in your constituency; ask your (Acting) Returning Officer for their details.

The nomination paper allows candidates to enter a 'description.' The description appears under your details on the ballot paper and indicates whether you are representing a political party, and if so which party.

If you are representing a party you can fill in the description, but it can only be: 1) one of the descriptions registered with the Electoral Commission, or 2) the registered name of the party. You must also supply a certificate of authorisation signed by your party's Nominating Officer.

(**NOTE:** If you are standing on behalf of a party and wish

to also have the registered party emblem printed on the ballot paper next to your name, you must sign and submit an emblem request form before the close of nominations.)

If you aren't representing a party you can either write the word 'Independent' (and/or 'Annibynnol' in a constituency in Wales) in the description box or you can choose to just leave the description box blank. If you leave the description box blank then the corresponding part of the ballot paper under your details will also be blank.

A Home Address Form
On the home address form you have to give your home address in full. If you don't want your address to be made public and to appear on the ballot paper then you have to state in what constituency your home address is situated.

Your Consent to Nomination Form
The third nomination form is a 'consent to nomination' form. On this form you're asked to give your date of birth and declare that you are both qualified and not disqualified from being elected. This form requires a witness.

If you have any doubts about how to fill in one of the nomination forms, check with the (Acting) Returning Officer or the Electoral Commission.

Timing & delivery of nomination forms
The nomination forms must be completed and submitted by 4pm on 'deadline day.' The deadline for becoming validly nominated will have been stated in a notice published by the (Acting) Returning Officer called the Notice of Election. The Notice of Election will say when (on what days) you can deliver the forms; note that the forms can only be delivered between 10am and 4pm on those days stated and that they can only be delivered in person by either you, your agent

(see below), your proposer or your seconder.

If you're in doubt about the arrangements for the delivery of nomination papers, check with the (Acting) Returning Officer.

The sooner you submit nomination papers, the better, as it'll give you time to submit a new set of forms if you've made any mistakes.

Deposit

By the deadline for becoming validly nominated you must also have deposited £500 with the (Acting) Returning Officer. The purpose of the deposit is to encourage only serious candidates to stand; it will be returned to you as long as you get more than 5% of the total valid votes cast in your constituency. Check payment arrangements well in advance with your (Acting) Returning Officer to ensure that there aren't any problems.

Election agents

Every candidate for a general election must have what is called an election agent. An election agent is legally responsible for the proper management of the candidate's election campaign. In particular, the election agent is responsible for all the financial aspects of the campaign.

You can act as your own election agent if you wish.

Free stuff

Validly nominated candidates get some things for free to help them inform the electorate about their candidacy.

First, candidates are entitled to free postage for one election communication to all the electors in the constituency. Contact a universal service provider such as Royal Mail to make arrangements for this, and for more information look at the Royal Mail's guidance on candidate mailings on their

website at www.royalmail.com.

Also, candidates are entitled to use certain rooms free of charge in order to hold public meetings. Such meetings can be held up until the day before polling day.

As ever, contact your (Acting) Returning Officer for more information on these topics if you need it.

Campaign publicity materials

During your election campaign you're going to want to produce materials – posters, flyers, advertisements and so on – that encourage people to vote for you. You should know that these campaign publicity materials are subject to a number of restrictions under electoral law and to the general civil and criminal law relating to published material. For example, no campaign publicity material may resemble a poll card or contain a false statement about the personal character or conduct of a candidate.

All your election publicity must also carry an imprint with the full name and full postal address of the printer and promoter of the material.

The Electoral Commission has produced further information and examples on this topic, and they're available for download at www.electoralcommission.org.uk.

Spending limits

As a candidate you're subject to spending limits during the 'regulated period' before the election. The regulated period runs from the date that you become a candidate until the date of the poll. After the election, you'll need to file an election expenses return with your (Acting) Returning Officer to prove you didn't breach spending limits.

Spending limits are a complicated area, and beyond the

scope of this book to explain in full. However, further information on spending, as well as donation controls, can be found on the Electoral Commission website at: www.electoralcommission.org.uk.

Campaigning

The idea behind an election campaign is to convince people to vote for you rather than one of the other candidates. Sound simple enough? In a way, it is. But a lot of work goes into a successful election campaign, and that goes double if you're standing in a marginal seat or one that's safe for another party.

We don't have the space in this book to exhaustively cover every detail of running a successful election campaign – that topic could easily fill a book all by itself, and indeed it has already filled hundreds of them – but we'll touch on all the important elements so that you have a good grounding in how to go forward.

A general comment

Much of an election campaign, besides educating the community on the issues, is about building relationships. If you can build a lot of positive relationships, and if in general you come across as a likeable candidate, then you have a great chance of success.

GETTING STARTED

If you're wondering where to start with your campaign, the best place is with a campaign committee and a campaign plan.

A campaign committee is a group comprised of your advisors. They should mostly be people that you already know and trust, but some may be new people that you recruit

specifically because of expertise they have in things such as 'the issues,' the media, political and electoral strategy, and finances. As much as possible the group should also reflect the diversity of the constituency. Your campaign committee should meet on regular basis.

Your campaign committee will be able to help you develop (and later implement) a campaign plan. A campaign plan is a document that indicates how you're going to get from point A (now) to point B (getting elected). It should break down your strategy of how you will get enough votes to win the election. It must include a timeline with all relevant dates and details of what you will do when. The peak of your campaign, as set out in your plan, should coincide with when you have the voters' attention, which usually means the week before polling day.

People you might need

Besides your campaign committee there are a few other people that you might need. If you have the money, a paid campaign manager – even a part-time one – is a great idea. You might have everything it takes to become a politician, but running a campaign is a skill all by itself, and it's too important not to give yourself the best possible chance by calling in an expert. A good campaign manager has excellent organising skills and a very good ability to work with people. They also need to be able to tell you when you are saying or doing something wrong (encourage this from everyone around you).

Also useful will be a treasurer to look after your campaign finances, and a volunteer coordinator (more on this subject below).

Canvassing

If you're lucky enough to be standing in a safe seat then it might not be required, but in any constituency that's even slightly marginal then canvassing, also known as 'legwork,' will be necessary. This means knocking on people's doors, introducing yourself, telling them you're a candidate, offering to hear what they have to say, and asking for their vote.

You'll need to figure out exactly how you are going to do your canvassing. Will you do blanket canvassing, or just target certain areas? Will you do it alone, with a group, or a mix? Use a map of the constituency and mark off completed areas as you go.

Take along cards or flyers with your name, something about the issues, and your contact information when you go canvassing. Whenever you come across a house where no-one is home, handwrite 'sorry I missed you' on it, sign it, and leave it under their door.

Take notes while you talk to people. It might very well be that a conversation you have ends up influencing a particular stance that you take on one of the issues.

Develop a list of people (with addresses and phone numbers) as you go who are definitely supportive of you, as you might want to call on them at a later date for assistance or make up the numbers at an event. If someone is particularly enthusiastic, ask him or her if they would like to get involved as a volunteer for the campaign.

Canvassing is campaigning at its most basic, but it's surprisingly effective – you'll find that people will remember conversations with you years later.

Meeting with and talking to community leaders
Meeting constituents one-on-one is necessary, but inefficient. Even if you convince every voter you speak with to vote for

you, there are only so many people you can meet in a day. Doing the same thing with community leaders however is highly efficient, as once on your side they will influence many other people to vote for you without you having to lift a finger.

So: seek out community leaders, tell them that you're standing for election, and offer to hear what they have to say. Even if there's no chance of them supporting you, ask for their views on your issues. Maybe they can't be persuaded to support your campaign, but doing this will help to 'neutralise' them and make them less willing to actively support someone else or talk negatively about you.

The Media

Campaigning inevitably involves dealing with the media, which can be daunting at first. Whole libraries have been written about how to deal effectively with the media, but a very short shortlist of dos and don'ts might look like this:

- Stay on message. Always know what you're going to say before talking to a journalist. Practice your campaign messages until they sound easy and natural.

- Keep your sentences short and direct. Don't ramble just to fill silences.

- Never give false information – the consequences if you're found out will be dire.

- Ensure that you're familiar with every media outlet before you are interviewed with them. Watch several episodes of a TV show, listen to several radio shows, read several issues of magazines and newspapers. Find out what their angle is and what they're likely to focus on.

- If you're asked about something you're not ready to answer, deflect it and get back to the message that you want to deliver.

- If you get asked by the media about a topic you don't know anything about, don't attempt to fake an answer. Admit you don't know, tell then you'll get back to them, and then do so.

Also note that many local newspaper editorial boards will endorse candidates. Once you have officially declared your candidacy, be sure to send information on your campaign to the editorial board. Ask them to meet with you so they can find out about your campaign directly from you.

Using the internet

The internet is a core element of modern political campaigns. Barack Obama's 2008 campaign for the United States Presidency featured the internet heavily. This naturally appealed to young people, as a natural result of using technology of which they are the heaviest users. The utility of his approach didn't stop there however: the embracing of social media created momentum which helped him build his visibility and credibility across demographic boundaries.

Obama's success has clearly influenced candidates, MPs and parties here in the United Kingdom. During the lead-up to the 2010 general election there was been a much more visible use of tools such as email, candidate websites, YouTube, Twitter, and social networking sites.

There's no doubt that you should embrace the internet during your election campaign. Here's a look at some of the best tools one-by-one:

- *A personal/campaign website.* A website is absolutely essential. It's the centrepiece of your online presence and should link to all the other tools that you use. When it comes to the design of your website, there's no need to reinvent the wheel, as there are already hundreds of good ones on the internet that you can use for inspiration (do

a search). A cheap way of actually getting your site built is to use an online freelancer through a website such as Elance (www.elance.com).

- *Social networks.* The biggest social networking site right now is of course Facebook (www.facebook.com), though others such as LinkedIn (www.linkedin.com) and MySpace (www.myspace.com) have their members too. Obama famously had a presence on sixteen social networks during his campaign. Facebook's functionality is perfect for a political campaign – you can have your own page with a news feed and your supporters can become 'fans.'

- *Twitter.* The micro-blogging site Twitter (www.twitter. com) allows users to post short, 140-character messages which are broadcast to everyone who subscribes to their feed. Twitter is a great non-annoying way to inform your supporters of upcoming events and to remain visible.

- *YouTube.* Video-sharing website YouTube (www.youtube. com) allows you to broadcast videos so that you can speak to supporters and constituents directly. Keep it very short and to the point though, and be aware that YouTube videos that miss the mark in some way get ridiculed mercilessly.

- *Email.* Email is both the most powerful and potentially the riskiest weapon in the online campaign arsenal. It's powerful because it's direct and therefore much harder to ignore than other mediums of communication on the internet. It's risky because if you abuse it people will hate you for it. For best results, use email sparingly, and only for when you want people to take immediate action.

When contacting supporters using internet tools, consider

little 'calls to action.' Ask supporters to change their Facebook profile picture and/or Twitter avatar to a campaign logo days before the election, or create and spreading a hashtag for when people Tweet about the campaign.

It's also important to use a cyclical message strategy. What this means is that every use of an internet tool includes links to others. Every YouTube video for example includes the URLs of the campaign website, the Facebook page and the Twitter page, and every Tweet links to YouTube videos and important updates on the Facebook page.

At the end of the day, 'old media' advertising such as television and print ads blanket a wide swath of voters, but with the internet you can target people much more effectively and for very little money.

Use of volunteers

Every good campaign requires volunteers to do the 'grunt' work. Some people will volunteer themselves, but others will need to be asked – don't be afraid to do this.

It's a very good idea to get a volunteer coordinator. A volunteer coordinator assigns tasks to volunteers, schedules them, coordinates group efforts and generally acts as a liaison between you and your volunteers. A volunteer coordinator needs to have good social, phone and computer skills. They should ensure that volunteers are comfortable with the tasks they're performing, provide training for volunteers where necessary, and organise snacks for the volunteers for when you have working bees (very important!).

You vs. the other candidates

Don't forget that standing for election means competing with other candidates for votes. You don't want to attack anyone, but you should get a good picture of your competition. A

good exercise is to list your strengths and weaknesses as well as those of the candidates. Then you can start to figure out how to draw attention to your competition's weaknesses while being ready to answer questions about your own.

Here are some areas to explore in your strengths and weaknesses lists:

- Political credentials and experience;
- Ability to motivate people;
- Access to resources;
- Availability of time to campaign;
- Health status;
- Employment history;
- Financial history, and
- Personal history.

Also, if there is an incumbent standing again, research his or her voting record in Parliament (use the website www. theyworkforyou.com). Does it reveal any weaknesses you could exploit?

Visibility

Being visible during an election campaign is of critical importance, so get out there as much as possible. Research events, groups and activities that you can attend. Ask everyone you know to tell you about meetings, events, pancake breakfasts, fairs and so on. Find out what community groups are doing and when and where they meet. As much as possible, be everywhere!

Besides your physical presence, you'll also need good pictures of yourself to go onto your literature. You'll need a simple portrait, but also get pictures of yourself doing things

like going door-to-door, touring the library, and inspecting the local recycling centre and so on. Don't forget to smile!

Issues
Issues are of course important. So what are the major issues that your campaign will focus on?

Generally it's best to choose three or four major issues that are important to you and to the people in the constituency. Focusing on just these will mean that people will be able to remember better what it is that your campaign is all about when they hear your name. A clear agenda is a very important piece of communication between you and the electorate.

Mail drops
We've talked about the internet, but what about a good old-fashioned mail drop? They're a good idea, but time yours so that it'll be read. People don't pay much attention to elections until right before polling day, so the weekend before the election is the most effective time for your literature to arrive in people's mailboxes.

Decide whether to do a blanket mail drop to everyone in the constituency or whether to restrict it to targeted areas in line with your campaign plan.

Keep in mind that studies have shown that people look at political campaign material for less than 10 seconds. This means you need to have immediate impact with the words, graphics and layout of your campaign literature if it is to do any good.

Creative campaigning
Don't forget to inject some creativity into your campaign so that you stand out from the crowd a little. You could hold a parade, dress in a silly costume for an event, plan a quirky

fund-raiser or draw some original cartoons to print on your literature. Things like this are fun for volunteers and bring a sense of humour and humanity to your campaign and to the issues. They can also help generate 'buzz' and create momentum for your campaign.

CHAPTER II
MANAGING YOUR IMAGE

INTRODUCTION

When Franklin Roosevelt was President of the United States, reporters and photographers collaborated with him to conceal the fact that he was confined to a wheelchair, and the vast majority of voters never knew he was paralysed from the waist down. Similarly, John F. Kennedy Junior used to cavort naked with women in the White House swimming pool, protected from prying eyes (including those of his wife) by staff and Secret Service agents. Again, the public had no idea.

Today, both of these feats of 'image management' would be impossible. Almost everyone carries tiny phones that take photos and videos, and those photos and videos can be broadcast to the world via the internet instantly and for free. One photo of Franklin Roosevelt in a wheelchair posted on the internet, or one video clip of John F. Kennedy Junior

naked in a pool with a secretary, and potentially career-ending consequences would have followed.

Technology has made managing your image more difficult than ever before, and one has only to look at the monotonous regularity of scandals, particularly sex scandals, in politics and public life both here and in the United States for proof.

This chapter, then, is dedicated to ensuring that your political career doesn't end before it has a chance to begin due to poor image management.

THE CONSERVATIVE NATURE OF PUBLIC LIFE

There is no job or profession more conservative than politics. Also, there is no other job or profession where you run the risk of being summarily sacked, with *no* legal recourse, for the mere suggestion that you might have breached those conservative rules of behaviour.

In a way, that's a good thing: it's entirely appropriate that public officials should be sacked for misusing funds or abusing a position of power. However, those 'conservative rules of behaviour' include sanctions for things that are really no-one's business but your own. Politicians have lost their jobs for behaviour that would barely raise an eyebrow if it was committed by someone not in public office.

By the way, you might decide that guarding your behaviour is too high a price to pay in return for attaining political office. If so, fine. But don't believe that it's possible to become a successful politician if you don't protect your image.

It would be nice if there the voting public weren't so hypo-critical. But this book is concerned with the world the way it is, not the way it should be.

Is this only something I need to worry about only once I'm a politician?
In a word, no. Certainly what you do while you're in public office, or while you're a candidate for election, is of greatest significance. Also, for past indiscretions you can get away with a certain degree under the heading of 'youthful misconduct,' but that's it. Digital recordings don't degrade over time, and the more successful you become, the more incentive there is going to be for people to dredge up things that you regard as ancient history. You need to start watching what you say and do as soon as you have made the decision to try to become a politician.

Things to avoid

These days, just about anything you say or do in public or *in private* could be visible to the public at a moment's notice. Ideally then, you would refrain from saying or doing anything that you wouldn't want broadcast. The list of things to avoid might look like this:

- Illegal drugs;

- Drinking to excess, especially in public;

- Any kind of sexual impropriety;

- Jobs (even part-time ones) of a questionable nature (stripper, nightclub owner etc.);

- Tax avoidance;

- Associations with infamous people;

- Any kind of 'sharp dealing' in your working life;

- Membership of political parties other than the major ones, and

- Membership of socially unacceptable groups.

Some of these things are illegal of course, while others are just distasteful or controversial. No matter: where possible, they are to be avoided.

Lifestyles

So far we've talked about isolated behaviour, but another aspect of the conservative nature of politics is that lifestyles that stray away from the norm don't go over well. Successful politicians are almost without exception married, usually with children. Single men are viewed with suspicion, single women even more so. And if you're a woman, even if you're married, having chosen not to have children will also count against you. Homosexuality, cross-dressing, not being married, nudism, being a hippy, alternative spiritual practices – all these and more may harm your chances of political success.

It's unfortunate that the true breadth and diversity of our society isn't represented in our politicians. But honestly, if you want to succeed in politics, you are best advised to present a 'normal' face to the world.

CHAPTER 12
DIFFERENT PATHS

For the most part, this book has assumed that you're at a fairly early stage of life, and that things such as university study and choosing a career are still ahead of you. But what if you're a little (or even a lot) further down life's highway? What if you've already been to university, already established yourself in a career, even had a family?

There no doubt that this changes things. Your best route into politics will be very different if you're 17 and deciding what to study at university, versus if you're 42 and have been working for 20 years in some other profession.

In a lot of ways however, the second scenario is easier. You don't have to decide what to study, try to get an internship, or pick the perfect pre-politics career. Older candidates tend to stand for election more because they are involved in the life of a particular place and want to represent it and be involved in helping to protect and improve it. And they tend to get preselected and then elected because people recognise this, and not because people think they're going to be the party's new star performer, so you aren't under as much pressure to fit that mould.

Rest assured that in its long life, Parliament has seen new MPs of every conceivable level of age and experience. On a purely anecdotal basis, people who know they're interested in politics from an early age tend not to get preselected or elected until around the age of at least 30. Age and experience count for a lot more than in other walks of life.

 how2become

APPENDIX I:
PRIME MINISTER BIOGRAPHIES

Below are the biographies of the current Prime Minster and of the four that immediately preceded him, from their school or university days up until when they became MPs for the first time.

The intention here is not to show you five journeys into politics so that you can pick one to slavishly follow. In fact, the intention is the opposite: to show you that there are many paths into politics even for those who go on to achieve its highest office. Hopefully you'll find them inspirational, or at the very least, food for thought.

DAVID CAMERON (2010-PRESENT)
Cameron studied Philosophy, Politics and Economics at Oxford and graduated with a first class honours degree. He then joined the Conservative Research Department and became Special Adviser to Norman Lamont, and then to Michael Howard. He was Director of Corporate Affairs at Carlton Communications for seven years.

A first candidacy for Parliament at Stafford in 1997 at the age of 31 ended in defeat, but Cameron was elected in 2001 as the Member of Parliament for the Oxfordshire constituency of Witney. He was promoted to the Opposition front bench two years later, and rose rapidly to become head of policy co-ordination during the 2005 general election campaign.

GORDON BROWN (2007-2010)
Brown was selected at a young age for an experimental fast stream education programme based at Kirkcaldy High School. He did well there and was accepted by the University of Edinburgh to study history at the age of just 16. He graduated from Edinburgh with First Class Honours M.A. in 1972, but then stayed on to complete a PhD (which he gained in 1982), titled 'The Labour Party and Political Change in Scotland 1918-29.' His political passion was emerging.

The fact that Brown attended the University of Edinburgh makes him one of only four university-educated Prime Ministers in history not to have attended Oxford or Cambridge.

While he was a student, Brown was elected Rector of the University of Edinburgh and Chairman of the University Court. He worked as a temporary lecturer at Edinburgh before lecturing in Politics at Glasgow College of Technology from 1976 to 1980. He then worked as a television journalist.

Brown joined the Labour Party in 1969 and was elected MP for Dunfermline East in 1983 at the age of 32.

TONY BLAIR (1997-2007)
Blair boarded at Fettes College, an independent school in Edinburgh, Scotland. After Fettes he spent a year in London, where he attempted to find fame as a rock music promoter. He then went to study jurisprudence at St John's College, Oxford.

Blair joined the Labour Party shortly after graduating from Oxford in 1975. During the early 1980s he was involved in Labour politics in Hackney South and Shoreditch.

He unsuccessfully attempted to secure selection as a candidate for Hackney Borough Council. Through his father-in-law, Tony Booth, he contacted Labour MP Tom Pendry to ask for help in pursuing a Parliamentary career. Pendry advised him to stand for selection as a candidate in a forthcoming by-election in the safe Conservative seat of Beaconsfield, where Pendry knew a senior member of the local party. Blair was chosen as the candidate. He won only 10% of the vote and lost his deposit, but in the process he impressed Labour Party leader Michael Foot and acquired a profile within the party.

In 1983, Blair found the newly created constituency of Sedge-field, a notionally safe Labour seat near where he had grown up in Durham. The branch had not made a nomination, and Blair visited them. Several sitting MPs displaced by boundary changes were interested in securing selection to fight the seat. With the crucial support of John Burton, Blair won their endorsement.

Blair was helped on the campaign trail by soap opera actress Pat Phoenix, his father-in-law's girlfriend. He was elected MP for Sedgefield later in 1983 at the age of 30.

JOHN MAJOR (1990-1997)
Major left school at age 16 in 1959, with three O-levels. He later gained three more O-levels by correspondence course, in the British Constitution, mathematics and economics. His first job was as a clerk

in the insurance brokerage firm Pratt & Sons in 1959. Disliking this job, he quit, and for a time he helped with his father's garden ornaments business. Major joined the Young Conservatives in Brixton at this time.

After a period of unemployment, Major started working at the London Electricity Board (where his successor as the Prime Minister, Tony Blair, also worked when he was young) in 1963, and he decided to undertake a correspondence course in banking. Major took up a post as an executive at the Standard Chartered Bank in May 1965, and he rose quickly through the ranks. He was sent to work in Nigeria by the bank in 1967.

Major stood for election to Parliament in St Pancras North in both general elections in 1974, but did not win this traditionally Labour seat. In November 1976 Major was selected by the Huntingdonshire Conservatives as its candidate, and he won this safe seat in the 1979 general election at the age of 31.

MARGARET THATCHER (1979-1990)
Thatcher went to school at Kesteven and Grantham Girls' School in Grantham, where she was head girl. She was then accepted to Oxford University, where she studied chemistry at Somerville College. While at university, kicked off her political career when she served as president of the Conservative Association. She earned a degree in chemistry in 1947 and went to work as a research chemist in Colchester and later in Dartford.

Only two years after graduating Thatcher made her first bid for public office. She ran as the conservative candidate for a Dartford parliamentary seat in the 1950 elections. She was defeated but earned the respect of her political party peers with her speeches. She tried again the next year but again was unsuccessful.

In 1952 Thatcher put politics aside for a time to study law. She qualified as a barrister in 1953. In 1959 at the age of 34 Thatcher finally won a seat, becoming the MP for the constituency of Finchley in London as a Conservative.

APPENDIX II:
GLOSSARY OF TERMS

Absolute majority: A voting basis which requires that more than half of all the members of a group must vote in favour of a proposition in order for it to be passed. This means that abstaining from voting is functionally equivalent to voting 'no.'

Administration: The organized apparatus of the state for the preparation and implementation of legislation and policies, also called bureaucracy.

Agenda-setting: Controlling the focus of attention by establishing the issues for public discussion.

Anarchism: A left-wing political ideology that calls for a stateless society that allows total individual freedom.

Authoritarianism: A system of government in which leaders are not subjected to the test of free elections.

Backbencher: Members of Parliament on the government side who sit on the backbenches and are not in Cabinet, or those similarly distant from Shadow Cabinet posts in opposition parties.

Ballot paper: A piece of paper with the names of candidates standing for election on it. The means by which voters cast their votes.

Bicameralism: A system of government in which the legislature is divided into two chambers, an upper and lower house.

Bill: A piece of legislation under consideration by a legislative body.

Bureaucracy: A type of administration characterised by specialisation, professionalism, and security of tenure.

By-election: An election held between general elections, usually because the sitting MP has died or resigned.

Cabinet: The Prime Minister and the most senior government ministers. The Cabinet constitutes the executive branch of government and is its ultimate decision-making body.

Cabinet solidarity: A convention that all cabinet ministers publicly

support whatever decisions the Cabinet has taken, regardless of their personal views.

Candidate: Someone putting themselves up for election with the hope of becoming the MP. Once Parliament has been dissolved, there are no MPs, only candidates.

Canvassing: Direct contact with voters by a candidate or their supporters during an election campaign. May be done for a variety of reasons, including assessing who voters intend to vote for, persuading them to vote a certain way, fundraising and so on.

Checks and balances: A system of government in which power is divided between the executive, legislative and judicial branches of government, and these powers check and balance each other.

Citizenship: Legal membership in a community known as a nation-state.

Classical liberalism: A liberal ideology entailing a minimal role for government in order to maximize individual freedom.

Coalition government: A parliamentary government in which the cabinet is composed of members of more than one party.

Coalition: When two or more parties agree to join forces and govern together, neither having the necessary overall majority in Parliament alone.

Common law: The accumulation of judicial precedents as the basis for court decisions.

Communism: A political ideology characterised by a belief in eliminating exploitation through public ownership and central planning of the economy.

Confidence: Support for the government by the majority of the members of parliament.

Conservatism: A right-wing political ideology generally characterised by a belief in individualism and minimal government intervention in the economy and society; also a belief in the virtue of the status quo and general acceptance of traditional morality.

Constituency: A physically delineated electoral district containing a body of resident electors who elect a single MP.

Constitution: The fundamental rules and principles, usually codified

in a written document, that people have made and agreed upon to enumerate and limit the powers and functions of a political entity,

Constitutional monarchy: A monarchy, such as the United Kingdom, where the monarch is largely a ceremonial figurehead subject to a constitution. Sovereignty rests formally with and is carried out in name of The Crown, but politically it rests with the people, as represented by a parliament.

Convention: A practice or custom followed in government although not explicitly written in the constitution or in legislation.

Coup d'état: A forceful and unconstitutional change of government, often by a faction within the military or the ruling party.

Deregulation: A government policy designed to remove regulations on market activity.

Despotism: An individual ruling through fear without regard to law and not answerable to the people.

Devolution: The delegation of powers to other parliamentary bodies within the UK, specifically, the Scottish Parliament and the Welsh and Northern Ireland Assemblies.

Diplomacy: A system of formal, regularised communication that allows states to peacefully conduct their business with each other.

Discretion: The flexibility afforded government to decide something within the broader framework of rules.

Dissolution of Parliament: The act of ending a Parliament. It is done by the monarch on the request of the Prime Minister.

Election: A formal decision-making process by which a group of people choose an individual to hold public office.

Election expenses: What a candidate spends on their individual campaign. Candidates are only allowed to spend a limited amount of money on their campaign, and accounts must be submitted after the poll proving they did not exceed this limit.

Electoral register: A list of all those in a constituency entitled to vote. Also known as an electoral roll.

Executive or executive branch: That part of government that has sole authority and responsibility for the daily administration of the state bureaucracy.

Fascism: An extreme form of nationalism that (historically) played on fears of communism and rejected individual freedom, liberal individualism, democracy, and limitations on the state.

Federalism: A system of government in which sovereignty is divided between a central government and several provincial or state governments.

First-past-the-post: An electoral system where each voter votes for one candidate and the candidate with the most votes wins. The simplest possible electoral system.

Free vote: A legislative vote in which members are not required to toe the party line.

Gerrymander: Manipulating constituency boundaries for partisan election purposes.

General election: An election at which all seats in the House of Commons are contested. General elections must take place at least every five years, but are usually held after about four years on a date chosen by the Prime Minister.

Government: The body with the power to make and enforce laws for a country, land area, people, or organization. In countries with Parliamentary systems such as the United Kingdom, also refers to the executive branch of the government; that is, the Prime Minister and Cabinet.

Head of government: The person in effective charge of the executive branch of government; the Prime Minister in a parliamentary system.

Head of state: An individual who represents the state but does not exercise political power.

Hung parliament: If after an election no party has an overall majority, then parliament is said to be 'hung.' The main parties will then try to form a coalition with one or more of the minor parties.

Ideology: A system of beliefs and values that explains society and prescribes the role of government.

Incumbent: At election time, the sitting MP in a particular constituency.

Independent: A politician or candidate who isn't affiliated with any political party.

Interest groups: Organisations whose members act together to

influence public policy in order to promote their common interest.

International law: The body of rules governing the relationships of states with each other.

International relations: An area of political study concerned with the interaction of independent states.

Judicial activism: The willingness and inclination of judges to overturn legislation or executive action.

Judicial review: The power of the courts to declare legislation unconstitutional (ultra vires).

Judiciary: The branch of government with the power to resolve legal conflicts that arise between citizens, between citizens and governments, or between levels of government.

Junta: A Spanish word meaning a group of individuals forming a government, especially after a revolution or coup d'etat.

Law: An enforceable rule of conduct.

Leader of the Opposition: The leader of the political party with the second-largest number of seats in the House of Commons.

Legislature: The branch of government responsible for making laws for society; the representative assembly which does so.

Liberal democracy: A system of government characterised by universal adult suffrage, political equality, majority rule and constitutionalism.

Limited government: A state restricted in its exercise of power by the constitution and the rule of law.

Lobbying: An activity of interest groups aimed at influencing governments and the public in order to achieve a favourable policy decision or decisions.

Magna Carta (Great Charter): A document signed by King John in 1215 conceding that the king is subject to law.

Majority government: A parliamentary government in which the party in power has over 50% of the seats in the legislature.

Marginal seat: A constituency where the gap, in votes, between the two or more leading parties is relatively small. Less than a 10% margin of votes (so requiring a swing of 5% or less in order to change hands)

is usually considered marginal.

Ministry: The entire group of MPs appointed by the Prime Minister to specific ministerial responsibilities.

Minority government: A parliamentary government in which the government party has less than 50% of the seats in the legislature.

Monarch: A person who heads a monarchy, for example a king or queen.

Monarchy: A form of government in which a single person (the monarch) rules under the law, usually for life. Note that a monarch may have unlimited power or may instead be only a ceremonial head of state with little or no power, with actual authority vested in a parliament or other body (as in a constitutional monarchy).

Monarchism: A political ideology in favour of a monarchy.

Multiparty system: A party system in which there are three or more major contenders for power.

MP (Member of Parliament): An elected representative holding a seat in Parliament. Strictly the term includes members of the House of Lords, but in practice it refers only to members of the House of Commons.

Nation: A group of people whose common identity (based on things such as shared common history, culture, ethnic origin and language) creates a psychological bond and a political community.

National interest: Interests specific to a nation-state, including especially survival and maintenance of power.

Nationalism: The feeling of loyalty and attachment to one's nation or nation-state.

Nation-state: A state with a single predominant national identity.

Official Opposition: In a parliamentary system, the largest of the opposition parties. The Official Opposition is given a special role to play in the legislative process and receives extra parliamentary funding in recognition of its status. They are a sort of semi-official 'government-in-waiting.'

One-party-dominant system: A party system in which there are political alternatives but a single political party dominates the political process as a result of the overwhelming support of the electorate.

Opposition: Those members of Parliament who are not part of the government of the day.

Parliamentary sovereignty: The supreme authority of parliament to make or repeal laws.

Party: [See Political party]

Party discipline: The convention that all MPs within any party vote together, as predetermined in the party caucus and enforced by the party whip.

Plurality: A voting decision based on assigning victory to the largest number of votes, not necessarily a majority.

Polis: In Greek, a city-state.

Political party: A political organisation that seeks to attain and maintain political power by putting up candidates to contest elections.

Political process: The interaction of organised political structures in making and administering public decisions for a society.

Politics: The process by which groups of people make collective decisions.

Polling day: The appointed day of an election.

Pork-barrelling: The practice of creating a policy that will benefit only the voters in one particular constituency even though all taxpayers will share the costs. Used by the party in government as a strategy for shoring up support in a marginal seat.

Portfolio: The administrative responsibility carried by a minister, usually made up of a combination of departments and other agencies.

PPC: Prospective Parliamentary Candidate. The same meaning as simply 'candidate.'

Preferential (alternative) ballot: Electoral system in which voters rank the candidates.

Preselection: The process by which a candidate is selected by a political party to contest an election for political office. Also referred to as 'candidate selection.'

Primary: An election in which voters in a constituency select candidates for a subsequent election. Primary elections are one means by which a political party nominates candidates for a general election.

A primary can be open to all registered voters in the constituency (referred to as an 'open primary') or may be restricted to members of the party concerned.

Private member's bill: Public bills introduced in the legislature by members who are not in the cabinet.

Privatisation: The sale of government-owned assets or activities to the private sector.

Progressivism: A left-wing political attitude favouring change or reform.

Progressive tax: A tax rate which increases as the amount of one's income increases.

Proportional representation: An electoral system in which the share of seats won closely matches the share of popular votes received.

Qualified majority: The raising of the simple majority requirement of '50% plus one' to a higher level, in order to protect the rights of the minority.

Reactionary: Political viewpoints that seek to return to a previous state in society. The term is meant to stand in opposition to and as one end of a political spectrum whose opposite pole is 'radical.'

Redistribution: The process of reallocating wealth and income to achieve an economic or social objective.

Redistributive tax: A tax that is intended to spread incomes more fairly among people, by taxing rich people more and poor people less.

Referendum: A decision on policy proposals by a direct vote of the electorate.

Representative democracy: A system of government based on the election of decision-makers by the people.

Responsible government: A form of government in which the political executive must retain the confidence of a majority of the elected legislature or assembly, and it must resign or call an election if and when it is defeated on a vote of no confidence.

Returning officer: The official in charge of elections in each of the constituencies.

Royal assent: The approval of a bill by the Crown.

Rule of law: A situation where all actions, of individuals and

governments, are (theoretically at least) subject to an institutionalised set of rules and regulations.

Runoff system: An electoral system in which additional rounds of balloting are held (with trailing candidates dropped) until a candidate receives a majority of the votes cast.

Safe seat: A constituency which is regarded as secured by a particular political party. A margin of 15-20% or more of the vote is usually regarded as safe.

Secularism: The idea that religion should have no place in government or any other aspect of public life.

Separation of powers: The separation of powers between executive, legislative, and judicial branches of government.

Shadow cabinet: Senior members of the Official Opposition whose job it is to scrutinise their corresponding office holders in the government, develop alternative policies, and hold the government to account for its actions and responses.

Single-member-plurality system: An electoral system in which the candidate with the most votes wins, even though that win may not represent 51% of the votes.

Single-party system: A party system in which there exists only one party and no political alternatives are legally tolerated.

Single transferable vote: A form of proportional representation in which electors vote for individuals rather than party lists, but they do so by ranking the candidates in their order of choice.

Socialism: A leftist political ideology that emphasises the principle of equality and prescribes public or common ownership of the means of production and social control of the distribution of income.

Social democracy: A left-wing political ideology in favour of reforming capitalism gradually, so that eventually socialism is arrived at but by evolution, not revolution.

Social justice: The partial equalization of wealth and income to reach a more desirable outcome.

Society: A self-sufficient group of individuals living together under common rules of conduct.

Sovereign: The highest or supreme political authority.

Speaker: An MP elected by other members of the House of Commons to chair debates and deal with the running of the House. By tradition, an MP who is Speaker is not opposed by any of the main parties at elections.

State: A combination of people, territory, and a sovereign government.

Statute: A specific piece of legislation.

Swing: A change in voter preferences from one election to another. Can refer either to an individual candidate or political party, or to a change in voter preferences between two or more candidates or parties.

Think tanks: Organisations that conduct research, engage in advocacy and attempt to influence government policy in a particular area.

Totalitarianism: A modern form of despotic rule in which the state undertakes to remake society according to an ideological design.

Two-party system: A party system in which there are two credible contenders for power and either is capable of winning any election.

Two-party-plus system: A party system in which there are two major contenders for power of approximately equal strength plus one or more minor parties able to win seats but not to control the government.

Tyranny: A form of government in which one person rules arbitrarily.

Ultra vires: Term used to describe an action which exceeds the conferred constitutional powers of the actor. Literally, 'beyond the power.'

Unwritten constitution: An uncodified constitution established through traditional practice.

Welfare state: The provision for redistributive benefits such as education and health services by the state.

Westminster: A term used to describe the hothouse of politics centred around the Palace of Westminster and its surroundings.

Whips: Officials in a political party whose primary purpose is to ensure party discipline in a legislature. They attempts to ensure that the MPs of their party are in attendance when important votes are taken and that they vote according to official party policy.

APPENDIX III
CONTACTING YOUR
ELECTORAL COMMISSION OFFICE

Within this section of your book are contact details for the various local offices of the United Kingdom's Electoral Commission (www.electoralcommission.org.uk):

- **London**
  Tel: 020 7271 0689.
  Email: london@electoralcommission.org.uk.

- **Eastern and South East**
  Tel: 020 7271 0600.
  Email: south@electoralcommission.org.uk.

- **Midlands**
  Tel: 02476 820086
  Email: midlands@electoralcommission.org.uk.

- **North of England**
  Tel: 01904 567990
  Email: north@electoralcommission.org.uk.

- **South West**
  Tel: 01392 314617
  Email: southwest@electoralcommission.org.uk.

- **Scotland**
  Tel: 0131 225 0200
  Email: infoscotland@electoralcommission.org.uk.

- **Wales**
  Tel: 029 2034 6800
  Email: infowales@electoralcommission.org.uk.

how2become

Visit www.how2become.co.uk to find more titles and courses that will help you to pass any selection process or obtain any career, including:

- How to become a magistrate.

- How to become a police officer.

- How to become a firefighter.

- Psychometric testing books and CD's.

www.how2become.co.uk